Discipleship and Society
in the Early Churches

Discipleship and Society
in the Early Churches

Thomas O'Loughlin

James Clarke & Co

JAMES CLARKE & CO

P.O. Box 60
Cambridge
CB1 2NT
United Kingdom

www.jamesclarke.co
publishing@jamesclarke.co

Hardback ISBN: 978 0 227 17736 5
Paperback ISBN: 978 0 227 17737 2
PDF ISBN: 978 0 227 90736 8
ePUB ISBN: 978 0 227 90737 5

British Library Cataloguing in Publication Data
A record is available from the British Library

First published by James Clarke & Co., 2022

For Verena
in gratitude

The years of our discipleship are threescore and ten,
and for the strong: fourscore (cf. Ps 90:10).

Contents

List of Illustrations

Unless otherwise specified, all photographs are the author's own

Acknowledgments

This book has been in preparation for almost a decade! It began life as a module on discipleship in early Christian texts for undergraduates in the University of Nottingham – and from the vigour and variety of their questions it took new directions and shapes on the five successive occasions I taught the module.

It also developed through various series of lectures I presented to those working in ministry in various churches in Britain, Ireland, Australia, and New Zealand. While the precise detail and terminology of their discussions changed from church to church, the deeper issues were, somehow, the same. For all the feedback I received from those groups I am very grateful.

I would like to thank my PhD students in Nottingham who often helped me sharpen my argument and, coming from a variety of Christian traditions, to draw me into areas where otherwise I might not have ventured.

I also wish to thank my friend and colleague Dr Patricia Rumsey for reading and commenting on the typescript, though the faults remain my own. I would especially like to thank Adrian Brink – his patience is a model for us all – who continued to believe in this book even when its author was more doubtful. And I would like to thank Samuel Fitzgerald who acted as its midwife in the process of publication.

T.O'L.
All Hallows Day, 2021

Introduction

Discipleship – Signing up for the Whole Package?

Walk through any town centre and you can get a quick but accurate picture of the situation in which the followers of Jesus find themselves today. There is a range of churches, from impressive buildings that have stood for centuries, to more recent buildings but whose shape and style cry out: 'this is a church'. There will also be modern buildings with clear modern branding declaring that they are churches, and a range of halls which also serve as churches. Some will be part of vast international networks, others will have far more tenuous links with a wider network, and some will be wholly independent. Some will have a whole backstory and a professional ministry – the clergy – while others will have a Bible, a hymnbook, and a pastor who is linked to just that group. If variety is the spice of life, Christianity is a very spiced religion.

However, for every church building that is still functioning, there will be others that are firmly locked or have been repurposed for other functions, such as shops, or have been taken over as mosques or gurdwaras as the ethnic make-up of the city has changed over recent decades. Go into most of the churches that are still functioning and you will notice that there is plenty of spare seating, and that many of the participants are greying. For most of their fellow citizens, religion is a matter of personal choice: one more optional interest. If you are 'religious', then this makes sense; but if you are not 'religious' then this whole array of churches is as irrelevant as a ballroom for someone who has no interest in dance!

These three features of modernity: (1) that there is no single form of Christianity that is taken as normative, (2) that it is widely seen as somehow past its sell-by date, and (3) that religious engagement is just an option, are now fully part of our western, developed-world experience. While we might want to note just how novel and how culturally specific these assumptions are, and might even want to regret them, what is important is that we take account of them as the background against which any study of discipleship takes place.

This trip around any western city and its many churches, church buildings, and ex-church buildings, however, only reveals one dimension of our situation. For apart from the buildings are the real churches – communities of people – who are energetic, dynamic, and looking to the future. These individuals and groups often express their vision of what it is to be a Christian not in terms of conforming to ecclesial pattern or membership of a club – both common ways of expressing a serious engagement with Christianity in the past – but in terms of being a disciple: discipleship, moving along a way as one committed to following Jesus, captures their sense of commitment, of engagement with the world around them, and their desire for a distinct set of relationships. In this process, they often turn afresh to the early churches and the earliest evidence we have of the followers of Jesus and their gatherings: churches. This book tries to take some themes of discipleship – as they emerge today – and then see how they are reflected in those early writings. Therefore, the starting point is discipleship today and then we look at how light is shed on that by the past.

This raises the immediate question: why not just produce a 'history of discipleship' focussed on the first and second centuries of the Common Era? The answer is simple: while there were many who were referred to as 'disciples' in those documents, and 'disciples' were a common commodity in the Graeco-Roman world where every philosopher and every teacher and indeed every master craftsman had some, the notion that one envisages one's religious engagement in terms of discipleship is a product of the twentieth century. It was only when a supposed 'Christian society' acted in such a manner that a Christian had to oppose it, tooth and nail, that the notion that being a Christian was more than 'belonging to a church' – or just identifying with some religious group – entered our world. Discipleship was not just passive identification, but taking one's commitment so seriously that it meant challenging church structures, the legal structures of the state, and even the accepted vision of society, despite most of that society having been baptised and a sizeable proportion of the members of that society being 'regular church goers'.

This was the situation in which many Christians found themselves in Nazi Germany where, unlike those Christians in the Soviet Union, as a state persecuted religion, they had to take a stand not only against the state but against the acquiescence of their fellow Christians who combined their church membership with their support, at least passively, for the state. Discipleship as a theme emerges with the Confessing Church in Germany during the Nazi era, and is linked to one name in particular: Dietrich Bonhoeffer. His 1937 book, *Nachfolge* (literally: 'following'), marks the moment when the theme entered modern Christian thinking. It was translated into English after the war with a title that captured its essence: *The Cost of Discipleship*[1] – and it came with the personal testimony that its author was willing himself to pay that cost. Bonhoeffer was murdered in Loewenberg concentration camp on 9 April 1945 as the Nazi regime crumbled.

To approach the topic of Christian origins from the standpoint of discipleship is to do far more than engage in an historical enquiry. It means to engage with the reality of the Christian past – for better for worse, warts and all – and then see if following Jesus is a worthwhile endeavour in the world in which we live today.

The Apprentices

So where do we start? We might begin with the notion of the apprentice who learns by doing. We have all heard the word 'disciple' hundreds of times. We even have very fixed ideas of what the disciples of Jesus looked like as they followed Jesus around Palestine on his journeys. It is just one of those words we use in church and do not think much about. But in the middle of the last century a group of Christians in Germany – faced with the horrors of Hitler's Nazis – became convinced that we needed to think about the whole matter once more.

It is very easy to think of our religion in terms of identities – and most situations encourage us to think in this way – so that I say 'I *am* a Catholic' or 'I *am* a Christian' or 'You *are* a Buddhist' or 'She *is* a Muslim'. The box is ticked, there is little more to say, and we can just see life as following accepted conventions (e.g. 'Jews go to synagogue' or 'Catholics go to mass') and that is that. But what if I recognised that becoming a follower of the Christ was not a done deal, but a work in progress? Now I would not start from my identity, but from my failure to recognise what being a Christian entailed, and I would become aware that at any time I might only glimpse what it means to be a disciple.

---

[1] D. Bonhoeffer, *The Cost of Discipleship* (London, 1955).

Lifelong Learning

It is very easy to get complete command of any body of facts that can be learned by rote, downloaded from a book, and then trot out predictable answers to old questions. What is far more challenging is learning slowly how to master a skill – whether this be the skills of a plumber or someone who seeks to build the Kingdom of God – because one must always be open to new problems, new challenges, and note that, while we are hopefully getting better, we are still far from perfect. One will only know one *is* a Christian at the end of a lifetime of trying to make life better, seeking to value love, seeking to minimise destruction, and seeking to bear witness to God the Father's love for all humanity manifested in Jesus the Anointed One. One is always *becoming* a Christian.

Growing and learning what it is to be a disciple is a *lifelong process*. Indeed, being a disciple is far more like being an apprentice in a trade than being a student in a school boning-up on a subject. The student has all the answers at hand if only she can get them all into her head; that done, she can pass the exam and 'be' something. The apprentice learns a bit here, learns another bit there, meets this situation and that, makes mistakes and has to start over – it's messy, slow, but is constantly in touch with the real world. Indeed, as the real constantly changes, the apprentice has to think up new solutions to problems that may never have existed before. If we think about Jesus being followed by his apprentices, and ourselves as his apprentices, then we radically alter our vision of who we are, what we are about, and what Christianity will mean for us today, and tomorrow.

Picasso, the painter, is reputed to have once said that 'tradition is having a baby, not wearing your grandfather's hat'. We often think of religion in terms of the past, and of holding on to the past, but if we are apprentices then the challenge is the future and making it a little more like the world of justice, peace, and love that God's love beckons us to build. Tradition is not a having, but a making. We hand on the vision of Jesus so that it is more there tomorrow than today.

Self-Image

If it is better to think of ourselves as apprentices to the Christ rather than being Christians, then each of the Sunday gospels challenges our assumptions, prejudices, biases, and certainties. Faith is an adventure to build the Reign of God, it is anything but our inherited 'old school' customs. The apprentice is always learning, and at the same time making a difference – hopefully for the better – to those around them.

Three Other Issues

You might ask why this book does not follow some systematic plan either of topics or texts? If one could reduce following to a plan it would be tantamount to saying that life is predictable. The skilled apprentice does not know just one or two patterns, but has to the skills to tackle problems that occur – and this book, therefore, follows a narrative sequence.

Very often historical works engage critically with the sources while works of theology/spirituality take a looser approach – but in fact modern human use an historically critical method in our everyday lives. When something goes wrong and there is an inquiry, that method is employed and it is by that method we seek to avoid falsehood, prejudice, and nonsense. It may not be an historical inquiry into the past, but its method is the same. Confronting the reality of what we know of our history is part of the challenge of discipleship.

This account is open-ended: it does not deliver a checklist, nor a package that can be absorbed over a certain number of training sessions. In recent years discipleship 'packages' and 'training programmes' have become big business: but that assumes that one can know our human nature far more fully than any sensible theologian is willing to admit. Life is open-ended in the calls it makes on us, and so is discipleship.

The Images

In this book you will find a series of images. They are not intended as 'illustrations' but as visual question marks. We often become so familiar with words that they become tired and we forget how challenging they originally were. Images too are often so familiar that that we take them for granted as part of our everyday background, but in their juxtaposition they can refresh and reveal one another. The eighteen images in this book can be seen as weaving in and out of the words in the chapters – drawing attention to points in a new way, refreshing them, or highlighting them. Meanwhile, the images themselves draw attention to the theological values that are virtually ever-present around us.

Chapter 1

Who were the Disciples?

Conflicting Expectations

The Starting Point

Religion is a source of conflict, strife, and needless confusion among human beings. This is a not a sentiment often found within the warm bubbles of believers of whatever make or shape, but for most people outside those groups, or within them looking from one bubble to another, the spectre of arguments is all too apparent. Even groups who, to outsiders, are all 'one sack, one sample' are often made up of sub-groups with the most vicious enmities over who are the true bearers of that religion's torch. Christianity has been splitting off groups since the beginning, suspecting the other as somehow corrupting, then demonising the other as 'heretical', and often taking that to its extremes. Christians of almost every shape have, in the name of the loving God and to preserve their loving loyalty to this God, used all sorts of physical violence – whether that meant the burning of theologians, the exclusion of 'the others' from an equal place in society, or the communal violence that needs 'Peace Walls' (topped with barbed wire) between denominations in Belfast. This would be just a social fact about human behaviour were it not that all these Christian groups transmit a rhetoric discordant with their actions. All claim that Christianity is the following of Jesus who is acclaimed as 'the prince of peace' (Isa 9:6), and they imagine themselves as followers of him who has 'reconciled all things, whether on earth or in heaven, by making peace through the blood of his cross' (Col 1:20).

Moreover, they say they are aiming at 'the freedom of the glory of [being] the children of God' (Rom 8:21); and when they assemble they imagine themselves as a fictive family addressing each other as 'brothers' and 'sisters' – though as early as the mid-first century these brothers and sisters were getting a reputation for quarrelling whenever they met up, as we hear in 1 Corinthians 1:11.

This awkward fact – that Christianity like every other religion can be a source of discord and division in our worlds – must form the immediate backdrop to any book on discipleship. If we want to write about what the following of a religious path meant or means, then we should do so in a subdued tone. We write with Auschwitz as our immediate backdrop, and know that we should recall the horrors of the 'otherings' involved in colonialism and racism – both justified in Christian language, then the seventeenth-century Wars of Religion in Europe, then ... and on and on. There is a painful truth that very few Christians like to acknowledge

Figure 1. A Maginot Line fort in northern France near Ypres.
This fort was built in 1938 and is just a recent example of how 'civilized' – and Christian – countries have related to one another over the centuries. It reminds us that human groups are more prone to suspecting one another than to being with collaboration. Discipleship of Jesus has to work against this endemic tendency.

about themselves: *the followers of Jesus have been, for much of their history, a group one would have been best advised to avoid* (if one could manage it). You might now find yourself thinking: 'that was not us, but them – them, over there and back then, who got the message wrong!' You are probably correct, but no one is insulated from the effects of past doctrinal arrogance. Rather than seek some basis for innocence, it might be more fruitful to look at the problem head on and see that all simple claims to have 'Jesus' message' need to be treated with scepticism. Significantly, this is not part of the self-image of most of contemporary Christians, but a book on discipleship, which needs to deal with group-images, must make this starting point plain.

Separations

Having named the backdrop, let us move closer to the topic in hand: discipleship. If division is a major element in the history of Christianity, then a contributing factor to factionalism is shifts in cultural values over time. Now the word 'disciple' (coming from the word *discipulus* in the Latin Bible) is a familiar word for most English-speaking Christians. It is seen primarily as a religious word – Jesus had the disciples around him – and is used, by extension, more widely of any group of dedicated followers. In these extended cases – as in phrases like 'the disciples of monetarism' or 'the disciples of Marx' – there is a certain note of blind devotion to a person or an idea. A kind of unreasoned following seems to be characteristic of a 'disciple'. The follower is not really thinking for herself. Indeed, one quick way to insult an academic is to declare that 'you are only acting as a disciple of …'. This brings the quick rejoinder that she is not the disciple of anyone, but has worked out the position for herself.

In this contemporary understanding of a disciple as not being a whole person, someone *pour soi*, one can see a difference between our culture today and those of the past. Today, we prize individual originality as a primary form of human excellence. Being a 'follower' is not a goal we set for ourselves. By contrast, for most of western history we have cases of writers who, rather than use their own names, were so desirous of being seen as followers that they presented their work to the world under the name and guise of the one they sought to imitate: hence all those ancient anonymous theologians whom we refer to with the prefix 'pseudo': such as the Pseudo-Philo, the Pseudo-Denis, the Pseudo-Augustine, or the

Pseudo-Jerome.[1] We tend to look down on pseudonymous writers as if they belong to the periphery – are they not actually pseudo-theologians (meaning 'false theologians' – simply 'fakes' or 'cheats') whose work is suspect? But what of the letters in the canonical New Testament which claim to be by Paul of Tarsus but which are of a later date and seek to present their teaching under the shade of his authority? What are we to make of the author of the Letter to the Hebrews, or the authors of the Pastoral Epistles, or, indeed, the authors of Colossians and Ephesians?[2] Shall we ignore these letters on the basis of the pseudonymity? The fact that we place a high price on the 'genuine' – seen as expressed in originality and individuality – shows that we have great difficulty in entering into the earlier mindset of disciples who 'passed off' their work as that of another.

This modern attitude can be seen in how we react to some historical statements. While most flee the desperate attempts of literalists 'to prove' such letters as the Pastorals are 'genuine' in the face of the evidence, many more are still troubled by the fact that disciples' letters are not as good as 'the real thing'. This can be seen in the frequency with which we use work-arounds such as 'the author of Colossians' or 'the author of Hebrews' rather than referring to their authors as 'the Pseudo-Paul'. A university student buying essays and passing them off as his own is seen as having committed the worse of academic crimes – and there are elaborate processes to catch such a student. But consider the ending of Hebrews:

[1.] To see the extent of this phenomenon in the world of Second Temple Judaism, see J.H. Charlesworth, *The Old Testament Pseudepigrapha* (London, 1983); and within early Christianity, see J. Machielsen, *Clavis Patristica Pseudepigraphorum Medii Aevi* (Turnhout 1990); and for an assessment, see T. O'Loughlin, 'Individual Anonymity and Collective Identity: The Enigma of Early Medieval Latin Theologians', *Recherches de Théologie et Philosophie Médiévale*, 64 (1997), pp. 291–314.

[2.] It would take us too far from our purpose here to examine in detail the arguments that point to these and some other letters as being of later origin than Paul of Tarsus. The most convenient way to get an overview of this scholarship is through the use of encyclopedic works; and in these cases see: V.P. Furnish, 'Colossians, Epistle to the' and 'Ephesians, Epistle to the', in D.N. Freedman (ed.), *The Anchor Bible Dictionary* (New York, 1992), vol. 1, pp. 1090–96, and vol. 2, pp. 535–42 respectively.

Pray for us, for we are sure that we have a clear conscience, desiring to act honourably in all things. I urge you the more earnestly to do this in order that I may be restored to you the sooner. Now may the God of peace who brought again from the dead our Lord Jesus, the great shepherd of the sheep, by the blood of the eternal covenant, equip you with everything good that you may do his will, working in you that which is pleasing in his sight, through Jesus Christ; to whom be glory for ever and ever. Amen. I appeal to you, brethren, bear with my word of exhortation, for I have written to you briefly. You should understand that our brother Timothy has been released, with whom I shall see you if he comes soon. Greet all your leaders and all the saints. Those who come from Italy send you greetings. Grace be with all of you. Amen. (13:18–25)

Is this the work of cheat, a con-artist who claims 'clear conscience' while passing off his own work as that of Paul of Tarsus, or should we look for a different attitude to the whole issue of identity? If the latter, then what the label 'Christian' and the notion of a 'disciple' meant for that culture might be very different from what they mean today. A crevasse has opened up between us and them, and until we stumbled upon it we imagined we were the ideal audience for those ancient texts.

Now consider another little writing, which we shall meet on several occasions in this book, with the title *The Training of the Twelve Apostles* (we will simply call it 'the *Didache*').[3] It is, like most 'how to' documents, not the work of a single pen or moment but something that emerged, expanded, and mutated over time: the actual text we read is the equivalent to a still taken out of a movie. Moreover, it is attributed to a very definite group within Christian memory – 'the Twelve Apostles' – but we know it is earlier in date than the formation of the that idea which combines two different groups: 'the Twelve' and 'the apostles'. Is it to be dismissed as a fraud because of this

---

3. The Greek text, with translation, can be found in M.W. Holmes (ed.), *The Apostolic Fathers: Greek Texts and English Translations* (Grand Rapids, MI, 1992), pp. 250–69, and also in B.D. Ehrman, (ed.), *The Apostolic Fathers* (Cambridge, MA, 2003), pp. 416–44; for an introductory study, see T. O'Loughlin, *The Didache: A Window on the Earliest Christians* (London, 2010).

title, or should we see the title as telling us something of the cultural values and situation in which it was used? As an anonymous, indeed pseudonymous, text, is its claim to 'apostolic authority' as serious a piece of deception (if it is deception) as the writer of Ephesians passing his letter off as written by Paul? Or is one a deception while the other is a piece of plagiarism? Do you see the matter as less serious because it is not in the canon – perhaps everything about this document is to be treated with less reverence than a text that is in 'the Bible'? The curious problem this raises is that none of the writers belonging to the rather amorphous group we refer to as 'the followers of Jesus' had any idea that they were writing such serious works or that their texts were to be put on a par with 'the scriptures' (what later Christians would refer to as 'the Old Testament'). Therefore, in placing their writings in this very special category – call it 'canonical' or 'biblical' – we are working with expectations that belong to us and our world, not to theirs. Yet another little chasm between our expectations and our ancient, inherited resources.

Rather than pursue 'the genuine' or 'the canonical', it is more useful to see what this phenomenon of pseudonymity tells us of the mind of those writers and their audiences. The simple difference in the tone of the word 'disciple' should alert us to the fact that, while we might read certain texts as precious to our identity – such as those texts that came to have canonical status for Christians and are known collectively as 'the New Testament'[4] – we do so within a different culture from that in which they were written. They belong to one world, we to another – and each world had/has its own expectations. It seems obvious that it is difficult to discover the implicit expectations of the ancient Mediterranean world – hence the work of historians and exegetes – but are our own expectations clear to us? We only discover our assumptions, our views of the world around us, with the greatest difficulty: it is in noting the discontinuities with other societies, such as those in the past, that we become aware of ourselves.

When we come to study discipleship and then turn to look at what we know of the first disciples, while we might wish to discover there a clear model and blueprint for today, we risk being disappointed by

---

4. It is worth noting how these questions often spiral off into a series of binary exclusions that prevent careful assessment of materials within the Christian tradition: thus 'canonical/non-canonical' is imagined to map on to 'inspired/not inspired'; then 'necessary/optional' and 'genuine/"pseudo"'; then 'early/later'; the 'definitive/opinion' or even 'true/false'.

what we find, or mistreating the texts to make them supply our needs. Moreover, when we see groups who imagine that they can simply take over what they find, ignore its own historical reality, and impose on it their expectations, we have to be suspicious. Reading a text, not written with us in mind, in a manner that assumes that it refers directly to our situation is the cornerstone of the phenomenon of 'fundamentalism'. It can be seen as a form of intellectual colonialism: assuming that something out there only exists, or has value, in so far as I take it over for my use. It is an activity of taking rather than respecting, enquiring, or dialogue. Fundamentalism is not confined to any one group of Christians nor to any one church – it is a pervasive human failing that sees everything in terms of current demands, certainties, and my needs. The Catholic who seeks to make an argument about the organisation of ministry today by an appeal to a notion that Jesus ordained twelve males at the Last Supper is engaging in the same form of historical colonialism as the Evangelical who expects, on the basis of a particular reading of 1 Thessalonians 4:17, 'the rapture'.[5]

Therefore, we start this inquiry with these two stark warnings. First, many Christians are wont to look at their history as if Christianity is – because of the claims they make about the significance of the Christ-event – a glorious golden path running through human history. This not only fails to address the facts of the situation, but also to respect those who suffered at the hands of people acting in the name of the Christ, and it creates a false sense of where they are now. A false view of the past usually produces a distorted view of the present. Second, while we study ancient texts as our inheritance and value them – for example in our liturgies – as 'the word of God', we must approach them from the standpoint of recognising that 'the past is a foreign country, they do things differently there'.[6] A failure to recognise that separation creates false expectations of the religious evidence with which we engage, and, in turn, creates problems in the present by taking badly formed insights as 'evidence'. It also obscures future possibilities from us if we do not acknowledge just how much of our 'now' can change because that 'now' is itself a cultural adaptation of the past.

[5.] See T.P. Weber, *Living in the Shadow of the Second Coming: American Premillennialism, 1875–1982* (Chicago, 1987).

[6.] See D. Lowenthal, *The Past is a Foreign Country* (Cambridge, 1985).

Our Past and 'the Past'

Christians, along with Jews and Muslims, are in a very complex place with regard to the past. From one perspective, the past cannot be ignored because it was in the past, at definite moments and in particular situations, that what is perceived as 'revelation' occurred. The life of Jesus, situated as it was within the historical situation of Second Temple Judaism, along with what was recalled as his preaching (of which the gospels are an expression), and the teaching of those who came in his immediate wake (such as Paul), is seen as foundational for later generations of Christians. That inheritance (whether it is seen as 'the scripture' or 'the tradition' within much later church formulations[7]) is seen as having a unique place in the lives of every Christian in every time and place. We can easily demonstrate this: can one imagine a Christian liturgy without some use of that inheritance in either reading or action or both? So, the inheritance, the past, matters.

From another perspective, that past is irrelevant and we can agree with Henry Ford: 'history is bunk'. Christianity is a relationship with God within a community and it demands a response to the situation now from within that situation. The focus of Christian action is the future. Thus, tradition is that which is happening now to bring about a more God-like future. In yet another perspective, Christianity recognises the divine as infinitely greater than the creation (classically expressed in the shorthand: *creatio ex nihilo*), and so all religious expressions are but moments, while the divine remains the goal that is ever greater. In such a perspective, we can cut free of history and engage in a theological quest that is akin to the philosophers' search for wisdom. Any one of these approaches is liable to yield distortions, yet holding them in equilibrium is a work of wisdom in itself.

Therefore, we hold on to history tightly but lightly. Tightly in so far as we must study it with great care, never forget it, and constantly return to it as a way of assessing our present; but lightly in so far as we must act wisely and as sensible, responsible people today (whatever past we might have inherited). This is not a dilemma, but an invitation to live with the paradox that the divine is greater than all situations, yet is to be found in particularities of place and time. We attend to the detail in order that we can ground our big picture. We look back at the past

---

[7.] This is another of those rather neat, but misleading, binaries – for a simple demonstration of the fallacy involved in such binary thinking, see D.C. Parker, 'Scripture is Tradition', *Theology*, 94 (1991), pp. 11–17.

Figure 2. Philotheos Bryennios.
While working in a library in Constantinople [Istanbul] in 1873 he discovered the text of the *Didache*. This was the first in a whole series of document discoveries (e.g. the Dead Sea Scrolls) that shattered the older notion that 'we knew all we needed to know' about Christian origins. Many questions about discipleship are open.

in its otherness from the present in order to relativise our present and speculate on alternative possible futures. Situations are always changing, our world is not the world of the past (even if we romanticise some past time as a 'Golden Age'), nor is faith a hankering after some lost 'age of faith' (if historical nostalgia is your 'thing', that is fine, but do not try to make it equivalent to faith), while our precious memories are not to be viewed as some ever-relevant paradigm for Christian action (you may like the idea that truth can be expressed in a written code – 'the Bible' – but your epistemological assumptions are not to be equated with faith). Moreover, the world that is coming to be – our tomorrow – will be different again. That said, looking at how Christians have acted in the past has the curious effect of freeing us to respond creatively in that tomorrow where disciples are asked to bear witness. The more we know of the past, the more we can cope with change now, and see possibilities for the future.

Finding the Key

There is a certain delight in getting to the heart of any problem, to the moment when you can exclaim: 'now I have got it!' Turning to the theme of discipleship there seems to be no end to the list of one-line or one-package answers. 'Discipleship' or 'discipling' – with the sense of 'to make someone a disciple' – is now a big business: one has to just look the word up on Google and see how many programmes, courses, and 'how to' books are available. The 'disciple of Jesus' is as clearly defined in lifestyle, aspirations, and attitudes as any ideal corporate employee.

There are training manuals, checklists, and schemes, all of which, usually over a very definite time-span and with very explicit learning outcomes, will turn someone into a disciple. It is a theological truth that Christians are made, not born; but in these 'programmes' one could say that 'disciples are produced' or even mass-produced. It is an approach that not only fits with our human desire to find a single, simple key, but aligns with much contemporary educational theory that one can package knowledge and skills, and then 'deliver' them. In this approach 'delivering a programme' is seen as synonymous with teaching, without recognition that its imagery is taken from the practicalities of logistics rather than the psychology of how humans grow.

One can make good soldiers, one can train good palaeographers, and can produce good computer experts, but 'making disciples' is a far more complex task. This is because discipleship touches the whole of our lives and each of us is different, our situations are as diverse as we are, and these are changing. Discipleship is up and down, calling for this, then calling for that, and it cannot be reduced to a package of skilled responses to a defined set of situations. However, if one looks at many 'discipling programmes' one can hear the marketers' pitch: use this and those you put 'through the programme' will achieve the outcome: they will be disciples! Not only – so go the marketing slogans – will this programme approach work, but it can be adopted as a package by your church or congregation through a corporate decision and then put into effect. Disciples are just a few clicks away!

While this is a prevalent approach today, it is not a new idea. Many founders of religious groups down the centuries have put forward the idea that there was a system, a method, or a 'rule' that could take the rather unruly 'material' that is human nature, with all the vagaries of individuals, and mould them into system that would produce some ideal Christian. A similar belief in systems of 'formation' animates the Catholic seminary system and has been adopted in the theological colleges of many other churches – and, despite the evidence of failure, they keep trying.[8] While these approaches are all very different, the underpinning notion is seductive and appealing: one can locate 'the pattern' of the ideal follower of Jesus, then build a system such that, if a less than ideal follower has the wit to enter it, the result will be transformation into that pattern. While it is a fact that such systems, both in the past and today, have helped many people, we should note that every such pattern

---

[8.] See C. McGrath-Merkle, *Bérulle's Spiritual Theology of Priesthood: A Study in Speculative Mysticism and Applied Metaphysics* (Münster, 2018).

is quickly replaced by yet another! Furthermore, as we shall see, *there is no single pattern of discipleship in the early churches* – or at least none that we can discern in the evidence that has come down to us.

A distinct, but similar, belief is that the content of the Christian proclamation – the *kerugma*: that which is proclaimed – can be expressed as a carefully worked out system. This desire also appeals to our human instincts which like ideas neatly bundled in a logical sequence, inconsistencies resolved, and loose ends tied up. However, when we turn to the historical record, we find almost the exact opposite: variety, variation, inconsistencies, lack of plan or coherence, and a hotchpotch of accidents. Closer examination of the evidence we have always had, combined with new evidence from such sources as the Dead Sea scrolls and the books from Nag Hammadi, reveal the amazing range of practices, beliefs, and ways of life of those who called themselves 'Jews' and of those who called themselves 'followers of Jesus' and eventually 'Christians'. Indeed, many today no longer refer to 'Judaism' (as if it were a monolith) or 'Christianity' (as if it could be reduced to a single pattern or body of doctrine) but to 'Judaisms' or 'Christianities'. This is little short of a revolution, and it affects how this book is written and how it should be read.

One of the most significant developments in the study of those around Jesus in recent decades has been the turn to plurality. For centuries it had been an axiom of scholarship that we could, and should, keep searching until we had identified a single, consistent original. This original state – be it a text, a practice, or a belief – would have normative status and from it we could trace changes, additions, subtractions, and deviations. Whether these mutations were viewed positively ('developments') or negatively ('corruptions'), they might all be traced back, by a process similar to working backwards along a genetic tree, to a moment in the life of Jesus, to an 'apostolic practice', to the author's pen of a canonical text, or to a moment when doctrine was not yet subject to disputes arising from mistaken interpretations.[9] But the work of Walter Bauer, in 1934, presented consistent and explicit doctrines as subsequent to a range of teaching,[10] while David Parker presented New Testament texts

---

[9.] See T. O'Loughlin, 'Divisions in Christianity: The Contribution of "Appeals to Antiquity"', in S. Oliver et al. (eds.), *Faithful Reading: New Essays in Theology and Philosophy in Honour of Fergus Kerr OP* (London, 2012), pp. 221–41.

[10.] W. Bauer, *Orthodoxy and Heresy in Earliest Christianity* (Philadelphia, PA, 1971) – but originally published in German in 1934.

as living responses to situations such that seeking 'the original Greek text' was a scholarly idol,[11] and Paul Bradshaw presented early liturgies as initially diverse with a standard 'shape' only gradually emerging rather than the reverse.[12] In one field after another, it has come to be recognised that chasing the unitary original reflects the hopes of modern church leaders and their theologians, rather than an attempt to understand the past. Therefore, in this book we are going to look at snapshots of discipleship – from a wide range of times and situations – and expect variety rather than prioritising that which could be seen as 'normative'. Discipleship always was, and still is, the very opposite of one-size-fits-all.

Why Bother with the Study?

Given that there is no master-plan for discipleship, nor is there any official manual, much less any executive summary, of what it means – with the possible exception of Matthew 22:37–39 which lacks detail – why study the hotchpotch of texts that have come down to us? The answer lies in the way we grow as human individuals. We are affected by the people, situations, and ideas we encounter on our journey. There is no single instant when we become Christians; we become disciples as a result of our encounters with others. It is in these encounters that we not only hear of the Good News, but grow in a relationship with others by forming a community of belief and lifestyle, with Jesus as the Christ by learning to pray with and through him, and with God whom we address as 'father'. These encounters are not just with the people we meet day by day, but within the events – the rituals of liturgy – in which we participate, with the ideas which we consider and call on in our actions, and the memories we ponder. It is these memories, and pondering them, that form the subject matter of this book.

I have not chosen to arrange the topics covered in an intellectually systematic manner (such as a God, then the Christ, then faith, then actions), but roughly in the historical order in which the texts were written. So, for example, Paul's churches had no experience of 'the gospel' as a text such as we find in Mark, while if we look at Mark's text we probably have something that was performed in a community that

---

[11.] D.C. Parker, *The Living Text of the Gospels* (Cambridge, 1997).

[12.] P.F. Bradshaw, *The Search for the Origins of Christian Worship: Sources and Methods for the Study of the Early Liturgy* (London, 2002).

had already heard a letter from Paul. Likewise, the churches that were giving their leaders very distinct status in the Pastoral Epistles were already familiar with the *Didache*, while there were several generations of Christians who used the *Didache* but never thought of their leaders in the way that these are presented in 1 Timothy. This approach – looking at the texts in a roughly chronological order[13] rather than within some thematic framework – is adopted for several reasons. First, we get a much better sense of what each text means when we read it in this order because we can see how contexts and situations were changing. The Christian self-understanding and the understanding of discipleship developed rapidly during the period before c.150 CE, and this approach allows us to appreciate this series of developments while alerting us to the dangers of reading texts anachronistically. Second, we rarely grow in our own understanding following a very clear systematic path – our growth is haphazard as we bump into this and then that. While formal teaching likes schematic programmes of logically linked ideas, most of what we 'pick up' about the ways we might live occurs informally – and this arrangement reminds us of that fact. Lastly, too often Christians have tried to present their inheritance – be it the collection called 'the New Testament' or a set of practices such as 'the sacramental system' – as if these are coherent, 'designed' programmes which carry an inherent sacral value. This tends to obscure the messiness we are actually dealing with as disciples in life, while it gives secondary aspects too much authority and prominence. By taking an arrangement that cannot make a claim to being programme, it may be possible to see the various parts of the inheritance in a fresh light.

These studies are presented as experiments in discipleship. They should not be seen as an attempt to provide some synthetic portrait of early Christian discipleship because, with our fragmentary remains, any such claim is at best an exaggeration. However, since we too are engaged, as individuals and groups, in our own experiments in discipleship, these may act as a mirror which can inspire and challenge us.

[13.] In recent years there have been several publishing ventures which seek to arrange the books of either the New Testament or the whole Bible in chronological order. The problem is that many of these texts cannot be dated with anything more than a rough sense of what is 'before' and what is 'after' – and, therefore, rarely do these ventures agree on a detailed sequence. However, the fact that they are produced reminds us that the collections are far more complex than a cursory glance at biblical titles and the period they claim to represent would suggest.

Chapter 2

A Community of the Covenant

Discipleship as Choices

Few literary scenes of a death are as well constructed as that of Moses in Deuteronomy. Slavery and escape, and the decades-long trek through the desert, were now in the past – banked as foundational memories of the people – and now, just on the brink of entering the Promised Land of milk and honey, Moses, great Moses, who had been God's instrument in this work, lies dying. And for the author of Deuteronomy there could not be a more fitting nor dramatic finale than a yes-or-no restatement of the pact between God and Israel.

> See, I have set before you today life and prosperity, death and adversity.
>
> If you obey the commandments of the Lord your God that I am commanding you today, by loving the Lord your God, walking in his ways, and observing his commandments, decrees, and ordinances, then you shall live and become numerous, and the Lord your God will bless you in the land that you are entering to possess. But if your heart turns away and you do not hear, but are led astray to bow down to other gods and serve them, I declare to you today that you shall perish; you shall not live long in the land that you are crossing the Jordan to enter and possess. I call heaven and earth to witness against you today that I have set before you life and death, blessings

and curses. Choose life so that you and your descendants may live, loving the Lord your God, obeying him, and holding fast to him; for that means life to you and length of days, so that you may live in the land that the Lord swore to give to your ancestors, to Abraham, to Isaac, and to Jacob. (Deut 30:15–20)

Rarely are options set out in such stark terms: 'life and prosperity, death and adversity' … 'life and death, blessings and curses'. And by the time of Jesus this had become one of those nuggets of memory that was seen to sum up God's challenge and invitation in a nutshell. There are two diverging paths: 'walking in [God's] ways' and 'being led astray'. You are on the move: which way are you going to take? This is the fundamental choice of discipleship: do you follow or not?

The formula, imagined as standing at a fork in the road, was so familiar in Second Temple Judaism that it had become proverbial religious wisdom and modern scholarship has given this commonplace a name: 'The Two Ways'. It can be found in any number of places in the scriptures, such as Psalms 1: 1–6 or 139:24 or Proverbs 2:13 and 4:18–19.[1] It is also found in those texts which were probably considered 'scripture' by the early followers of Jesus (but which later were excluded from our canons) such as 1 Enoch 94:1–5 or 2 Enoch 30:15 (42:10). It survives in other Jewish literature, and is found in Qumran in *The Community Rule* in the form of the choice of 'the paths of justice and truth' whose followers are animated by 'the spirit of patience, generous compassion', versus 'the paths of darkness and evil cunning' taken in 'a spirit of deceit' which lead 'to eternal damnation'.[2]

It would be inconceivable that such a well-known device for presenting the relationship with God would not be used, and then probably adapted, by the followers of any late Second Temple rabbi such as Jesus. Our earliest evidence for this use is the first, and longest, section of the *Didache*. It begins:

There are two ways: one is the Way of Life, the other is the Way of Death; and there is a mighty difference between these two ways.

---

[1] See K. Niederwimmer, *The Didache: A Commentary* (Minneapolis, MN, 1998), pp. 59–63, for a much fuller list of parallels. The formula is much older than the Book of Deuteronomy, but by the time of Jesus the location in a book of 'The Law' would have been seen as its original and paradigmatic source.

[2] 1QS 3:13–4:16; see F.G. Martínez, *The Dead Sea Scrolls Translated: The Qumran Texts in English* (Leiden, 1994), pp. 6–7.

> The way of life is this: first, you shall love God who created you; second, your neighbour as yourself; all those things which you do not want to be done to you, you should not do to others. (1:1–2)

This is followed with a long series of what to do ('Give to everyone who asks help from you, and do not seek a return because the Father wants his generosity to be shared with everyone', 1:5) and what not to do ('Do not be fickle or deceitful because the deceitful tongue is the snare of death', 2:4). Then we get a description of 'the Way of Death':

> Now, by contrast, here is the Way of Death.
> First, it is full of wickedness and is cursed: it is full of murders, adulteries, lusts, acts of fornication, robberies, acts of idolatry, magic and sorcery, thefts, false accusations, sham, double dealing, fraud, arrogance, malicious intentions, stubbornness, covetousness, obscene language, jealousy, haughtiness, pride and pomposity. (5:1)

And then a pen picture of those who choose that way, which concludes:

> These people do not know who was their Maker.
> They are murderers of children, they are corrupters of God's image, they turn away from those in need, oppress the afflicted, are advocates of the wealthy, treat the poor unjustly.
> All told, they are full of sin! (5:2)

The formula, sometimes with the image of the choice of ways and sometimes as just a stark set of commands and prohibitions, has survived down to our own day. My own favourite modern example is an imaginary map produced by Charlotte Reihlen in the nineteenth century titled 'the broad and narrow way'.[3] The image reduces a many-layered religious language to a single horizon of meaning: two *post-mortem* destinations presented as outcomes of directional decisions starting just outside a local town. Everything that is fun, from dancing to sport on Sunday, lies along the way towards death, while those going towards life seem to have a rather dull time of hymn singing and Bible study.

[3.] C. Reihlen, *The Broad and Narrow Way* (London, 1885) – it had many variants from the 1860s onwards in several languages; and can easily be found of the web by searching for 'reihlen broad narrow way'.

THE BROAD AND NARROW WAY.
Matthew VII. 13, 14.

Figure 3. Detail of the Two Ways on Reilen's map.
It has been a constant temptation to present the path of discipleship as
a series of fixed, well-defined steps. The popularity of this map was partly
due to the manner in which it made following the narrow way a matter of
very straight-forward choices in a manner similar to those who would
resolve ethical issues by asking 'what would Jesus do?' Life is rarely
so straight forward.

While Reihlen's 'map' now looks like a curiosity, the basic image – one
road upwards towards a glorious destination; one downwards towards
darkness – with its deceptive simplicity is still a standard item for those
who believe that discipleship can be packaged. Sometimes the package
is even less imaginative and presented as a series of tick-boxes. Then if
you check every item in the 'do' list and also tick 'no' in the 'avoid list',
you can proceed to the next step: you have 'qualified' as a disciple.

Perspectives

While 'the two ways' is an ancient formula still familiar to us, the
question arises if our current perspective in approaching it would
have any parallel in the world in which it arose – for the same text can
have radically different meanings when transposed from one culture

to another. One way to observe this difference is to ask who is the 'you' in the question 'you must decide between the way of life or the way of death?' In answering this, the first problem is to realise that it is a genuine question. Most people reading the *Didache*, or looking at its modern analogues, just take it as a matter of personal, individual decision. Indeed, there is no more to it than that: how could there be? If you see a tick-box on a questionnaire asking 'Do you pay tax?' and 'Are you over 18 years of age?' you do not even have to think about it: you answer for yourself. It is information about you as a single individual not about any group to which you might belong. Likewise, faced with this command: 'you shall not practise with magic potions' (*Didache* 2:2), you acknowledge your acceptance, and it becomes the imperative for your own actions: 'I will not use magic potions.' But in a pre-modern, non-western world such individualism is rare: individuals act (obviously) but do so in terms of the group to which they belong. A very simple way to see this is to look again at Deuteronomy. Moses is presented as addressing Israel – the people as a whole. It is the people who have to come into a binding relationship with God, not just a collection of individuals who all happen to have taken the same option. When Moses is not addressing the whole People of God – 'speaking all these words to all Israel' (Deut 31:1) – he is addressing and blessing the tribes (Deut 33). When the formula is used in Qumran, it is the community that is addressed – it is the rule of the community as such – rather than just individuals who happen to be there. And in the *Didache* the individual who is addressed as 'my child' (e.g. at 3:1) is one who is being instructed before baptism by a member of the community on what is the lifestyle of the community that will become the fictive family of that person when baptism occurs.

We place a massive emphasis on the personal – it is my choice – and see this as the only way to be genuine and authentic; by contrast, all of the texts on discipleship from ancient Judaism and Christianity suppose that one joins a group as a disciple. One can only be really 'one of them' when you are part of, accepted by, and in harmony with a group. The next step is thus to think about individualism – and how it affects religion.

'Individualism' was a notion first mentioned in the mid-nineteenth century by Alexis de Tocqueville in his reflections on American society, when he described it thus:

> Each person, withdrawn into himself, behaves as though he were a stranger to the destiny of all the others. His children and his good friends constitute for him the whole of the

human species. As for his transactions with his fellow citizens, he may mix among them but he sees them not; he touches them, but he does not feel them; he exists only in himself and for himself alone. And if on these terms there remains in his mind a sense of family, there no longer remains a sense of society.[4]

In this perspective only the individuals are 'really real' and clubs, associations, co-operatives, groups of friends – anything which is a team activity for humans – not to mention any notions that we are social animals, society, or humanity – are just accidental and secondary. This individualist view sets up a polarity between the individual and the society – and in such a polarity the individual has to look out for herself or himself (and, if lucky, strike a deal for mutual non-aggression and perhaps for even better trading with those around). We should not imagine this view as particularly new – some have always taken this view but were labelled misanthropes – but since the later Middle Ages it has become ever more acceptable not only in society but within religion. We think of devotion as a most intimate affair – which it is – but then extend that to the notion that it is, *therefore*, a completely private matter. Not for us the need to travel to the Temple in Jerusalem – a central motif in our accounts of Jesus[5] – and we find John 4:21–24 ('the hour is coming when you will worship neither on this mountain nor in Jerusalem ... and those who worship [God] must worship in spirit and truth') much more conducive, but fail to notice that it is framed in terms of communities – Jews and Samaritans – and that such excluding divisions between communities are overcome in the time of the Christ.

We utter again and again the word 'covenant' or speak of our relationships with God, but do not note that our ancient documents speak of God having chosen a *people*, and so the relationship is with that community rather than 'us', a collection of individuals who happen to have the same perception about God's presence in their lives. This intellectual, cultural, indeed psychological, distance between then and now – what I call the 'shift in perspectives' and which in terms of the

---

4. A. de Tocqueville, *Democracy in America* (New York, 1945), p. 318.
5. The three Synoptic Gospels arrange their narrative around a trip that ends in the Temple in Jerusalem, while John has Jesus going up to the Temple on three occasions (from which mentions we have traditionally derived our idea that Jesus' ministry lasted three years).

history of ideas could be termed a 'paradigm shift'[6] – constitutes one of the primary challenges of Christian believing today. We want, more than we like to admit, to be 'rugged individuals' in our religion, yet disciples as we read about them are more than just loners in the same school. They form 'the school'. The school – all those disciples together – is the reality and the disciple is a part – a member of this bigger body and cannot exist apart. The part depends for its existence on the whole – and the whole is more than the sum of its parts. This (for many today) is surely overstating the case against individualism! So perhaps it is time to read again this passage:

> Indeed, the body does not consist of one member but of many. If the foot would say, 'Because I am not a hand, I do not belong to the body,' that would not make it any less a part of the body. And if the ear would say, 'Because I am not an eye, I do not belong to the body,' that would not make it any less a part of the body. If the whole body were an eye, where would the hearing be? If the whole body were hearing, where would the sense of smell be? But as it is, God arranged the members in the body, each one of them, as he chose. If all were a single member, where would the body be? As it is, there are many members, yet one body. The eye cannot say to the hand, 'I have no need of you,' nor again the head to the feet, 'I have no need of you.' On the contrary, the members of the body that seem to be weaker are indispensable, and those members of the body that we think less honourable we clothe with greater honour, and our less respectable members are treated with greater respect; whereas our more respectable members do not need this. But God has so arranged the body, giving the greater honour to the inferior member, that there may be no dissension within the body, but the members may have the same care for one another. If one member suffers, all suffer together with it; if one member is honoured, all rejoice together with it.
>
> Now you are the body of Christ and individually members of it. (1 Cor 12:14–27)[7]

---

6. See T.S. Kuhn, *The Structure of Scientific Revolutions* (3rd edn, Chicago, 1996).

7. This passage should be read in conjunction with the larger argument: 1 Cor 12:12–31; and compared with Rom 12:4–5 where Paul also uses this parts-of-the-body parallel.

Entering Another World

The notion that we live and understand within 'a world' – or a 'construct' or a 'worldview' – that we have to leave in order to enter that of the early followers of Jesus seems far too complicated for many, and they default to letting the texts mean what they want them to mean. It is useless to argue with such a position or simply to declare it inept or label it with a term like 'fundamentalism'. A better approach is to notice that we all find passages that we claim to respect, even treasure, such as that just given from Paul, which we 'cannot get our heads around'. This sense of 'I cannot get my head around' usually has little to do with stupidity and quite a lot to do with the fact that what we are reading belongs to a different world. Just as we often 'cannot get our heads around' the values or decisions of societies that seem far from our own, so the odd item from the early Christian times that we cannot get our heads around alerts us to its foreignness. These moments should then put us on our guard: what else is going on that I do not understand whose strangeness has not even struck me?

The process of getting our head around this sense that discipleship is a group-thing, and that we have to have a sense of corporate personality as our framework for reading texts such as Deuteronomy (in the way it was used by Jesus and his followers), Paul, those who formulated narratives about Jesus (gospels), and their community structures, is a slow one.[8] But here are three starting points.

Fishing was an important industry on the Sea of Galilee, and many of the first disciples were fishermen – there are over 30 references to fish and fishing in the gospels – but we should also recall that it was a corporate activity.[9] Whether they were fishing from a boat, from the shore, or some combination, this required very precise teamwork. One man could not fish, nor could each own their own nets, nor could a boat be operated by an individual. The manner in which the members of these groups were related – be it a co-operative or as employees – is less significant than the

---

[8.] The classic study of this was H. Wheeler Robinson, *The Christian Doctrine of Man* (Edinburgh, 1911) and 'The Hebrew Conception of Corporate Personality', *Beihefte zur Zeitschrift für alttestamentliche Wissenschaft*, 66 (1936), pp. 49–62.

[9.] See F.D. Troche, 'Ancient Fishing Methods and Fishing Grounds in the Sea of Galilee', *Palestine Exploration Quarterly* 148 (2016), pp. 281–93, for a detailed account of how organised groups of people were needed for the forms of fishing that they pursued.

fact they were mutually dependent and this gave them an appreciation of belonging within a unit that would starve or survive that is very different from our experience. Such ancient groups were keenly aware of their interdependence and the need to look out for one another. We mainly experience such teamwork when playing sports – and these are cases of opting-in voluntarily to the team – but ancient workers grew up with this understanding of how work/survival required becoming part of a larger body, and they did not have an option if they wanted to have food for themselves and their families. Now, recalling that to be a fisherman was to be part of a group of fishermen who could work in very precise ways together in what could be a dangerous physical operation, we can appreciate better this opening memory of Jesus calling disciples as found in Mark:

> As Jesus passed along the Sea of Galilee, he saw Simon and his brother Andrew casting a net into the sea – for they were fishermen. And Jesus said to them, 'Follow [*deute*] me and I will make you [*humas* (note the plural: ye)] fish for people.' And immediately *they* left *their* nets and followed him.
>   As he went a little farther, he saw James son of Zebedee and his brother John, who were in *their* boat mending the nets. Immediately he called *them*; and *they* left their father Zebedee in the boat with the hired men, and followed him. (1:16–20, my italics)

While we tend to think of it as a scene of individuals, the wording of the story is set in the plural. 'Follow' (*deute*) is a plural command which we would have to represent in English by a phrase like 'You guys! Come and follow me.' Jesus then says that he will make them (i.e. Simon and Andrew) into a new kind of fishermen – and so they followed Jesus. Likewise, James and John are in a family business with hired men working with them, but it is as a pair of brothers that Jesus called them. This is just an incidental detail in Mark's story, but it shows up for us a very definite different perspective on individuals/groups. Mark was not seeking to make a specific point, nor should we imagine that time as one of communitarian bliss, but simply note how we respond to these texts from such an individualistic point of view.[10]

---

10. Curiously, if one looks at the adverts seeking to recruit ministers used by some churches (e.g. the Roman Catholic Church uses them extensively and calls them 'vocations' adverts') they interpret this scene exclusively in terms

A feature of many languages, including English, is that we transfer the names of human gatherings, actual groups with an identity, to the place or building in which they meet. Thus, we think of a 'college' as a building or place used for educational purposes, having long forgotten that it is the gathering of the teachers and their students. 'The council' is often the place where that group meets or the responsibilities they discharge, while we say 'I walk to the university' and think of a place rather than the group who make it up. Now consider two words we meet in both the New Testament and in the Greek translation of the Old Testament (the 'Septuagint'): 'synagogue' and 'church' (*ekklesia*). When we hear these words our first thought is of buildings: one is used by Jews (and when we hear this in the gospels as in Mark 1:21, '[Jesus] entered the synagogue and taught', our image is of him going through doors into a building – and indeed visitors to Capernaum today are shown the much later synagogue building there and told: 'this is the place where Jesus stood and taught'); the other building is used by Christians (though sometimes as when we hear 'tell it to the church' (Matt 18:17) we might realise that a church is an assembly of people *before* it is the building in which they assemble). But consider these two statements:

> And the Lord said to Moses,
>   'Say to all the congregation of the people of Israel, Ye shall be holy; for I the Lord your God am holy' (Lev 19:1–2).[11]

> Then Moses spoke the words of this song until they were finished, in the ears of all the assembly of Israel:
>   'Give ear, O heavens, and I will speak; and let the earth hear the words of my mouth.' (Deut 31:30–32:1)

---

of individual 'special calls' without any reference to the collective nature of discipleship/ministry.

[11.] Note the command is in the plural: it is the people who should become holy. Modern translations, knowing that 'ye' has disappeared from ordinary English usage employ 'you' in the command 'you shall be holy' – this is grammatically correct in that English now uses 'you' for both the singular and the plural, but we are apt to read it as a singular addressed just to me the reader, whereas it is addressed to a community. If 'ye' sounds too dated, then it needs to be translated with 'You all shall be holy, because I, the God of you all, am holy.'

In the first quotation the word for 'congregation of Israel' is *synagoge* in Greek, while in the second the word of 'assembly of Israel' is *ekklesia* in Greek. 'Synagogue' and 'church' are, in effect, synonyms for a gathering, a group, people collected together with something in common linking them into a distinct group. In Palestine there is little or no evidence for distinct synagogue buildings at the time of Jesus (though there were such community centres in the diaspora),[12] but even where there were such special buildings where our canonical gospels would have been heard (e.g. the islands of the Aegean) the word synagogue would have been heard first as a collective noun before it was heard as pointing to an edifice.

We have a rather dismal way of demonstrating that 'synagogue' evoked a group rather than a building from two verses in the Book of Revelation where there is mention of 'a synagogue of Satan' (Rev 2:9 and 3:9). The author wants to distinguish between 'those who say that they are Jews and are not, but are a synagogue of Satan' (2:9) and it is clear that being a member of a synagogue is to be understood as belonging to a group. This is a dismal verse because it was used by later Christians to set up the faulty and dangerous opposition of 'synagogue versus church' and 'Satan versus God' that has so disfigured the Christian action – not to mention the understanding of the dependence of Christianity on Judaism – that forms the dark backdrop to the Holocaust. Returning to our main topic here, once we think of 'synagogue' as a religious gathering we are in a position to reread many other texts, such as, for example, this one: 'And [Paul] entered the synagogue and for three months spoke boldly, arguing and pleading about the kingdom of God' (Acts 19:8). The exact significance of what Luke wants to convey becomes clear if we render it as: 'And [Paul] entered the assembly and … spoke boldly.'

This problem of confusing a group with its building might have confused some Greek Gentile followers of Jesus who heard Paul or Apollos or Mark, but the word *ekklesia* would not. For them 'church' – since they did not have special Christian buildings – had no hint of bricks and mortar, nor did it have any connotations of an ecclesiastical apparatus, but meant only an assembly to which they had chosen to belong. For us, it is a word that often occludes as much as it illuminates – and we then forget that belonging to a group was in antiquity a key to survival.

---

12. See E.M. Meyers, 'Synagogue', in D.N. Freedman (ed.), *The Anchor Bible Dictionary* (New York, 1992), p. 255.

This leaves us with two curious questions. First, if 'synagogue' and *ekklesia* were synonyms among the Greek-speaking Jews among whom Christianity as we know it took root, why did the word *ekklesia* become so associated with Christianity to the extent that it was seen to exclude Jews? The key point to make in answering this question is that we do not really know and we have no means of coming to a definite answer because the use of *ekklesia* for the gathering of the Jesus-followers is already taken for granted by the time of our oldest sources. Paul's earliest extant letter is addressed 'to the church of the Thessalonians' (1 Thess 1:1), it is also found in the Two Ways section of the *Didache*: 'You should acknowledge your transgressions in the church; and you should not set out on your prayers when you have a bad conscience' (4:14). Much ink has been spilled over trying to see some subtle shade of meaning distinguishing one word from the other – but such speculation is misplaced in that it assumes that Jesus' early followers were all as interested in subtle linguistic shifts as a group of theologians sitting in a university seminar room: in ordinary life we do not use words with such rigorous attention to verbal subtleties. A popular explanation is that it is a case of wanting a deliberate distancing from Judaism using a linguistic see-saw: 'if you call yourself X, then we will call ourselves Y'. This explanation is certainly wrong because the break-up into two distinct, later antagonistic, camps had not yet taken place, and all concerned would have known that there were many virtually interchangeable words in Greek for a group/club/assembly/party/gathering/congregation.... Perhaps it was as simple as the word *ekklesia* being used once, then others repeated it, and it became the accepted name for a particular group of people who met to discuss the significance of Jesus' teaching – and the name stuck. Some reject this because it seems too accidental, too happenstance, but history is full of such acts of a moment becoming normative: just look at the number of people today who rejoice in calling themselves 'Christians', yet the word originated as a slur by the Roman authorities to identify a potentially seditious group they were seeking to identify. The use of 'church' (and then later the use of 'church'/'synagogue') may be a parallel case.

The second question is why do we use the words 'church' and 'synagogue' in our Bibles when both are now distracting (to buildings) or confusing ('synagogue' still has negative undertones and can feed anti-Semitism; 'church' conjures up a power group: the clergy)? Would it not be simpler and better to use a word like 'assembly' or 'gathering' or 'assembled gathering' instead (and in the case of 'synagogue', when it is clear that it also refers to a building, to use 'community centre')?[13] The answer is clearly yes – the aim of translation is to convey the meaning of the text and seek to explain one culture within another. But we must not be naïve: religion is for many people a deeply nostalgic affair and a way of thinking that they can recapture the past – to such people words are like little charms and they are more interested in warm feelings of familiarity with yesterday than understanding with an eye to today and tomorrow.

The key point for us is that these words (synagogue/church/ synagogues/churches) are used nearly 180 times in the canonical New Testament, and when they were first heard these words would have called up group images and suggested the notion of belonging or not-belonging within those groups.

The last example of how we perceive individualistically when earlier disciples would have imagined collectively concerns a text most readers of this book could recite by heart. The Lord's Prayer is known to virtually every Christian. Its origins are far more complex than the origin story created by Luke (Luke 11:1–14), but what is not in doubt is its importance in the communities of Jesus-followers from as early a time as we can reconstruct.[14] We are so familiar with an individual, private, piety where others are almost intruders into our authenticity – and especially our notion that responsibility for evil, crimes, and misdemeanours is an matter of finding singular culprits – that we simply do not hear the words we recite in this prayer which is wholly devoid of 'I' and 'me' any 'my' and 'mine'. It is worth rereading it just to watch for all the plurals:[15]

---

13. I owe this translation of 'synagogue' as building to Meyers, 'Synagogue', p. 253.

14. See D. Clark, *The Lord's Prayer: Origins and Early Interpretation* (Turnhout, 2016).

15. The reader might object, rightly, that this traditional form – sometimes labelled 'the reciting text' – is a faulty English translation of a defective second-century Latin translation and should be replaced with a more accurate form. It is used here not because it is accurate, but precisely because as the reciting text it is still the form most familiar to the greatest number of those who know the prayer by heart.

Our Father	– not: *my* Father
who art in heaven, hallowed be thy name, thy kingdom come, thy will be done on earth as it is in heaven.	
Give *us* this day *our* daily bread.	– not: give *me my* daily bread
And forgive *us our* trespasses,	– not: forgive *me my* trespasses
as *we* forgive those who trespass against *us*.	– both the forgiveness and the victimhood are collective
And lead *us* not into temptation, but deliver *us* from evil.	– both trial and safety are imagined in terms of the group where we belong
For thine is the kingdom and the power and the glory, now and forever.	
Amen.	– this is a group response giving their affirmation in liturgy.

The assumption in this prayer is that one is standing in the midst of the group praying; and that if that group is not there, then one is still praying within a virtual group. This is the way that the prayer is mandated in the *Didache* (8:2–3); the way it is presented as part of the group's perspective in Matthew's gospel (6:9–13 – note the plurals in the opening: 'Ye all (*humais*) should pray like this'); and in Luke it is imagined as Jesus responding to a group request from the disciples that they as a group of disciples would be taught to pray as group just as John the Baptist had taught his followers.

A Vision of Society

If we succeed in becoming aware of the gap between our perspectives and those of the early disciples of Jesus, then what difference does it make to a text like the Two Ways that they saw as such a key to discipleship that it was worth committing to memory? The stark difference is that it is no longer a private list which I use to measure private behaviour as if I were in an examination, and it becomes a vision which the group has of their society and for their society. The individual usually knows when they have erred (and if someone is immune to such awareness the checklist will make little difference), but a group needs a vision of what makes a good life, a healthy society, and to have an ambition towards which they strive. Moreover, if they believe in God as the creator, then they need a crisp picture of the sort of world that God wants for his people and so the sort of world they should be striving to build. We need to read the Two Ways as just such a vision of society: this is the sort of place we want to live in; this is the way we want people to relate one other. Each of the disciples contributes to the vision knowing that when they act individually that it is each 'doing her/his bit'. This – all good actions are parts in a vision of society that is identified as God's people – is caught in the vision of the coming of the Son of Man in Matthew's gospel. Each good action – such as giving food to someone who is hungry – is seen as being done directly to Jesus, but those gathered from all nations at his right hand speak with one voice as a community: 'when did we see you [Jesus] hungry or in need?' and the reply comes: 'Truly, I say to you all (*humin*), as *ye* did it to one of the least of these my brothers and sisters, *ye* did it to me' (Matt 25:40).

Following the Way: the Challenge of Balance

Not only is the Two Ways document a community vision – their desire for a society that was part of the covenant/new covenant/new testament – but being saved is not the image of a loner being picked out of the sea, but a whole new people rejoicing in God's goodness. The communities that heard the gospel being preached saw this as their distinctive hope and imagined that they would be the group who, through the way they acted out their vision, would be at God's right hand. Discipleship was to join in the larger endeavour with those in your assembly.

Does this group/community/whole people view of salvation not remove the challenge of discipleship from individuals? Ironically, it does the exact opposite. Then as now, there is a balance to be struck between the individual and the group. Whether in our personal actions or in our theoretical constructs, it is always easier to swing out to an extreme. In our personal actions it is usually to the extreme of individualism that we are drawn, whereby we decide to look after 'Number One' (and our own) at the expense of the group, humanity, or, as our generation has recognised, the planet. The Jewish and Christian traditions are full of warnings: be it the story of Cain versus Abel, the Rich Man with Lazarus, or later variations on this such as Dickens' Ebenezer Scrooge. Discipleship involves moving beyond self, me, and mine. Theoretically,

Figure 4. The doorway of the parish church in Colliour in southern France.
The addition, above the door, of the the the name of the French Republic and
the motto of the Revolution was probably made in a spirit of antagonism
to 'the church' by a state who saw its values and those of the church as
contradictory – and certainly 'the church' was usually happy to be
identified as being opposed to all that the revolution stood for. A little
further reflection should have reminded the church members that
liberty, equality, and brotherhood were basic ideas in discipleship.

it means that the extremes of capitalism and socialism – which mutually
support one another as extremes – are attractive in their simplicity, but
both reduce the individual (be it to a component or consuming unit)
and reduce the society (be it to public squalor amidst private excess or
to a juggernaut devoid of human-scale values).

Even in the realm of religion these extremes are attractive. On one
side is the notion of a set of tick-boxes – mainly of actions to avoid –
which lead to 'being saved' or another set of boxes which if I can fill
them – with specific 'good works' – gets me an entrance ticket to bliss.
On the other hand, there is the notion that, so long as the group, 'the
Holy Church', is preserved, then we can skip over any damage such
corporate thinking created for individuals. The balance – valuing the
individual and valuing the common good – is the hard road.

That discipleship involves a commitment to the common good is perhaps the aspect of discipleship that is least attractive to many people – and, indeed, there are many who boast the name 'Christian' who seek to dismiss it in favour a private-focussed, inward-looking religion which sees such concerns as simply the intrusion of a political theory into theology. However, the very distinction that is here used is one that belongs to modernity rather than the cultures or times in which Judaism and Christianity arose.

The notion of a loving God who created us for a community and who then entered into a covenant with a people is another way of stating that the concern for the common good is hard-wired into us as God's creatures. Likewise, it takes account of the fact that we are only fully human as individuals when we are engaged within a community of love and with a society that values both what is private and what is common. Thus the disciple cannot simply value her/his own freedom, but must be aware that so long as there is a slave anywhere, there is a challenge to oppose this. One cannot only provide for self and the immediate group while there are others in need whom one could assist – or all, both as individuals and as a society, are demeaned and I share responsibility for the damage. If anyone is oppressed, I am oppressed – and may be to blame to a greater or lesser extent.

Discipleship along the way of life as a complex balance of valuing both the individual and the common good is not a new problem. When William Wilberforce (1759–1833) recognised that the slave trade was incompatible with Christian faith, he was ridiculed by many Christians for stepping beyond the realm of discipleship into the world of the economic common good.[16] So few Christians in France at the time of the French Revolution recognised human fraternity as a Christian ideal

---

[16.] Catholic moral theology textbooks in the United States defended the compatibility of owning slaves with Christian belief until the American Civil War. See F.P. Kenrick, *Theologia Moralis* (Mechelen, 1860), tract 5, ch. 6 (*De servitute*), nn. 35–41. Just on the eve of that war, a Catholic priest visited John Brown on the night before he was executed and tried to defend slavery using quotes from St Paul and his treatment of Onesimus (Phlm) – to which Brown replied that he did not care what St Paul did, but what he said, and not even what he said if it was in favour of slavery! See J.W. Ely and D.P. Jordan, 'Harpers Ferry Revisited: Father Costelloe's "Short Sketch" of Brown's Raid', *Records of the American Catholic Historical Society*, 85 (1974), pp. 59–67.

that the slogan of the revolutionaries, *liberté, égalité, fraternité*, was perceived as an attack on religion. Indeed, there are many Christians today who do not see movements for freedom or justice as having any connection with their beliefs.

Discipleship within a covenant community often looks as if it can be reduced to simple choices – picked off a list – but in reality it is far more difficult. This is why disciples are expected to spend a long time learning from their master – and it is foolish for us to imagine that we have moved beyond the status of learner. Training and formation are always slow and partial – hence Paul's statement that love is greater than our now partial understandings (1 Cor 13:8–13).

Chapter 3

'The Sons (and Daughters) of the Light'

At the End of History

Having observed that discipleship is a group activity – one is a disciple among other disciples, and one becomes a disciple by being inducted into a community – it seems that the next question we should ask is: what was it like to be a member of such a group?[1] Here again we run into the problem that the first followers of Jesus have left us so little material that we have to use historical reconstructions – engaging our imaginations to move from fragments and bits to pictures – to try to answer our questions. To get some sense of how these men and women perceived themselves as disciples we have to examine our earliest sources which make reference to the community and ask: what sort of community would elicit that sort of comment from a teacher such as Paul – whose genuine letters are our oldest roughly datable sources – writing to that community. While this is both indirect, partial, and just one point of view, it is both the best we can do and does not pretend that Christian discipleship can be boxed-up as a neat package.

Now, of the surviving 'genuine' letters written by Paul (as distinct from those written in his name), it is widely assumed that the text we know as the First Letter to the Thessalonians is the earliest we have and dates from

---

[1] The quotation in the chapter title is from 1 Thess 5:5.

around 50 CE.[2] The letter as we have it is probably a combination of two shorter letters to the church in the city,[3] but for our purposes here we can treat it as a single unit. The reason why many suspect that our letter is a combination of several shorter missives is that at 4:1 Paul says 'Finally' – the marker of being about to conclude – but then picks up steam again for some completely new material. What is perhaps most significant about this is that it reminds us that we must not treat these texts, even when they have the hallowed ring of being in 'the Bible', as complete and perfect. All our information about the first disciples is patchy and we know little about how these letters were treated in the early communities. We know that there are other lost letters of Paul, and those we have may be very different from the text that he committed to a traveller with the request that it be taken to a particular community and then read aloud to them.

Thessalonica in Paul's time was, as now, a great port: the trading gateway between the Balkans and the world, linked by shipping routes in the Aegean and the Mediterranean more widely. That there was a Jewish community, a synagogue, there is beyond question, and this would have been Paul's first destination when he arrived in the city. Curiously, the letter that we have is not addressed to any Jews who chose to follow Jesus, but to a community that had 'turned to God from idols to serve the living and true God' (1:9). This conversion was only possible for Gentiles – what later Christians would refer to as 'pagans' – for Paul, along with all his fellow Jews, had no place for idols or polytheism and all worship was directed to the true and living God. So here we have a letter that is explicitly aimed at Greeks, Macedonians, who have come directly to the kind of discipleship preached by Paul without having imagined themselves 'ordinary' Jews or else were so recently converts to Judaism that it was still part of their memory that they had abandoned the many gods worshipped in the city (and whose remains in the form of temples are still to be seen in archaeological excavations in the city today) before hearing Paul and his companions. Did Paul not gain any followers among the Jews in that city? The simplest route to an answer to this might be to turn to Luke's Act of the Apostles where there is an account of Paul's arrival and stay in the city (17:1–15).

Luke tells us that there was a synagogue and that Paul and Silas, as usual, went there and argued for three weeks about the scriptures and the identity of Jesus. 'Some of them were persuaded ... as [were] a great

---

[2.] R. Riesner, *Paul's Early Period: Chronology, Mission Strategy, Theology* (Grand Rapids, MI, 1998), pp. 364–6.

[3.] J. Murphy-O'Connor, *Paul: A Critical Life* (Oxford, 1996), pp. 104–10.

Figure 5. St Paul: 'Preacher of the Truth, Teacher of the Nations'.
This is the classic image of Paul with a large two-edged sword – a visual allusion to Hebr 4:12 ('The word of God is … sharper than a two-edged sword'). Paul's inherited image – e.g as the author of Hebrews – is very different from what emerges from a critical study of the genuine letters. Many positions (e.g. on 'grace') that have been identified as 'Pauline' for centuries need to be reassessed in the light of modern scholarship – and this is often a disruptive process for churches.

many of the devout Greeks and not a few of the leading women' (17:4). But other Jews were jealous and complained to the city's authorities that Paul was causing serious trouble and presenting Jesus as a rival king to the emperor. As a result, 'the brothers' – those who had chosen to accept Jesus – had to arrange the departure of Paul and Silas by night to Beroea, but the troublesome Jews of Thessalonica followed Paul and caused more trouble for him there (17:13). At first sight this would explain our letter: the Jews apparently remained Jews and it was the Gentiles who accepted Paul's message. This would account for Paul writing to 'the Thessalonians' as a church made up of Gentiles who had turned from their idols. However, this is not an adequate explanation for several reasons.

The first source of dissatisfaction is that we can only use Luke's account of what actually happened in Paul's time with great circumspection. While it claims to be almost a blow-by-blow account of the apostle's activities, it was written at least half a century after the events and we cannot ascertain how accurate Luke's information was. Moreover, Acts has a very definite theological vision of its own, a view of a providence guiding each moment in the mission, and this account of events in Thessalonica fits that account. This does not mean that the events narrated are not accurate, but it equally means that they cannot be taken for granted. The second reason for placing only limited value on Luke's account is that it is not internally consistent. Luke begins by telling his audience that *some* of the synagogue were persuaded – so there were some Jewish disciples of Jesus there – along with others from the wider population, but then gives the impression that it was a simple dispute of Jews versus disciples of Jesus. This supposes a clarity of group identity that made perfect sense in Luke's own time but is not applicable to Paul's time. This raises the possibility that we have here an instance of his 'evidence' being no more than a circle of inferences. While the extent of Luke's acquaintance with Paul's letters is controversial, it could be that Luke's account is his attempt to make sense of the fact Paul wrote to a Gentile community of disciples (those who had 'turned from idols') whereas Luke knew that the place Paul would have started was in the synagogue.

However, there is a simpler explanation for the details of the letter as we have it and which takes account of Paul's obvious starting point within the synagogue. Paul made disciples among both Jews and Gentiles, and, as we would expect, they became disciples with very different histories/community memories and with very different expectations of what 'the gospel' meant for them. The extent to which these disciples could actually interact is an open question. Perhaps they met together and recognised a common bond in 'the gospel' but perhaps it was only a very notional sense of a common hope. One could speculate about a Gentile being willing to accept something new, but not liking the idea of being associated with what was a sect within the city. Likewise, one can imagine a Jew who can accept that 'the gospel' is also for the Gentiles but who finds their social habits foreign and repulsive. Likewise, one can envisage that the questions and problems arising from discipleship of Jesus would be very different in each group. What was just the familiar language of Jewish expectation about the end times would not have been problematic for the Jewish followers of Jesus, but it would have been socially and politically disruptive for Gentile followers. Such differences would explain our letter.

The whole group of disciples in Thessalonica was divided on ethnic lines: those of Jewish ethnicity along with converts of longer standing to Judaism who had now chosen to follow Jesus; and those Greeks who had moved directly from the smorgasbord of practices that made up 'Graeco-Roman religion'. This latter group had specific difficulties in relation to what Paul had said about the end times and it was to this group – not to all the followers of Jesus in Thessalonica – that he wrote. Did this mean that the Jesus-followers had separated out into distinct groups/churches? We simply do not know. It could be that there were there, as we know there were in Corinth, separate factions within churches. Churches were, in any case, small groupings – they could fit in a house – and so it could be that people filtered to where they felt they were with those of similar background: such 'sticking with your own' is a basic human default. It could be that they met together but had fundamentally different visions so that they could barely understand one another – and consulted Paul who recognised that the questions were a concern for only one section and he replied to them. However we imagine the groupings of Jesus-followers in Thessalonica, one thing seems clear: this letter is not to all of them, but only to a specific group about problems that affect that group.

Where then did Luke in Acts get the idea of a straightforward them–us dispute? It could be that he was trying to make sense of what Paul wrote in 1 Thessalonians 2:1–16. There Paul refers to making 'the gospel of God' known in spite of 'much opposition' (2:2). But is this 'opposition' from Jews in Thessalonica as Luke suggests, or is the issue more complicated? It is clear that Paul's Gentile converts have suffered, but there is no statement by Paul that this is from Jews. He is quite explicit: just as the Jewish disciples of Jesus in Judaea have suffered at the hands of Jews who have not become Jesus-followers, so you (Gentile) followers have suffered from 'your own countrymen' (2:14). Paul is pointing to a similarity of experience between different groups – Jesus' followers face persecution – rather than a single continuous phenomenon. Moreover, when he says that 'they hinder us from speaking to the Gentiles' (2:16) it is not clear whether these are Jews who do not accept Jesus or whether they are Jews who are Jesus-followers but who hold that his message was intended only for Israel. On balance, it is most likely the second alternative: this is the group based in Judaea that Paul mentions elsewhere who accept Jesus but do not think of Jesus' teaching as being for the uncircumcised/Gentiles.[4]

Why is this important for our understanding of discipleship today? When many Christians today hear parts of this letter in a liturgy it comes with the opening: 'A reading from the first letter of St Paul to the Thessalonians', while others open their Bibles and see a similar heading: 'The First Letter of Paul to the Thessalonians'. This conveys the image of every Christian in the city gathered in one place with the unity of newly converted zeal, reinforced by persecution from without, who are going to hear/read this letter which is itself a carefully crafted communiqué

---

4. This is the party of the circumcision that Paul mentions in Gal 2 (and elsewhere in that letter: e.g. 6:15); and which caused Paul to oppose Cephas/ Peter to his face when the latter went to Antioch (Gal 2:11).

of profound theological truths that are as relevant now as then. But the reality is almost the very opposite. The letter is only aimed at the very specific questions of a community within the group of Jesus-followers there and it is what makes them different from other Jesus-followers in the city that elicits Paul's words. Not only are the letter's contents contingent to this situation, we find that the letter is unclear at many points (since we only know part of the story) and it is all too easy to over-estimate the level of our understanding. If there is a religious point being made by Paul in these opening sections of the letter it is that disciples of Jesus should be ready to face opposition from those who are around them because that seems to be the reaction that they provoke whatever their background. But can disciples today 'take a lesson' from these passages? Perhaps it is this: difference of opinion and sectioning into smaller groups is an ever present reality among communities of disciples. Therefore, instead of deepening these differences into opposing camps, each claiming an exclusive understanding and possession of the way, they should recognise that not every disciple of Jesus has the same questions, problems, or inheritance – and that an integrated and harmonious community is a goal they should all be working towards rather than seeing themselves as 'on the way' and the others as deviants, those who have departed from the way.

The response of Paul to the problems of this group of Gentile disciples in Thessalonica also raises other issues for us.

The Gospel

One of the striking features of the opening sections of 1 Thessalonians is the way that Paul uses the word 'gospel'. He does so on no fewer than six occasions:

> because our gospel came to you not in word only, but also in power and in the Holy Spirit and with full conviction (1:5)
>
> but though we had already suffered and been shamefully mistreated at Philippi, as you know, we had courage in our God to declare to you the gospel of God in spite of great opposition (2:2)
>
> but just as we have been approved by God to be entrusted with the gospel, even so we speak, not to please mortals, but to please God who tests our hearts (2:4)

> So deeply do we care for you that we are determined to share with you not only the gospel of God but also our own selves, because you have become very dear to us (2:8)
>
> You remember our labour and toil, brothers; we worked night and day, so that we might not burden any of you while we proclaimed to you the gospel of God (2:9)
>
> we sent Timothy, our brother and co-worker for God in proclaiming the gospel of Christ, to strengthen and encourage you for the sake of your faith (3:2)

Even on a cursory reading it should be clear that what we today mean by 'gospel' or 'the gospel' and what Paul means is not the same. Indeed, some translations are so struck by how strange these verses sound that they change a phrase like 'entrusted with the gospel' (2:4) to 'entrusted with the message of the gospel' which seems to make much more sense.

To most Christians today 'the gospel' is primarily a message, 'good news', or the content of the teaching of Jesus. Thus, we speak of 'gospel values' and mean something like an ethical code that is in harmony with the preaching of Jesus. Sometimes we still use it in a binary of 'law' versus 'gospel' with a hint that one message has succeeded another, earlier less perfect message: but even for those who reject the implicit faulty theology in such contrasts,[5] the gospel is still one message about God contrasted with another. However, by far the most common understanding is that it is the name of a kind of book, such as 'the gospels' found in the Bible or one of 'the apocryphal gospels' (not in the biblical canon) or the text read at the liturgy: 'a reading from the holy gospel according to …'. By extension, we get 'evangelists' who wrote gospels (and now proclaim the message of these books, 'evangelicals' as those who like to imagine that they stay close to these books, and 'gospel music' which is song somehow connected to these books). None of this is of any help in understanding Paul who had died before there was any text to which we would give the name 'gospel'.

The primary meaning of the word *euaggelion* is derived from imperial politics. It was an agreement between the emperor and some political entity, usually a city, that a relationship of dependency, loyalty, and protection existed between them. The city promised loyalty to the emperor and acceptance of his rule, and in exchange it received the

---

5. See M.M. Boulton, 'Supersession or Subsession? Exodus Typology, the Christian Eucharist and the Jewish Passover Meal', *Scottish Journal of Theology*, 66 (2013), pp. 18–29, for an exposition of implicit supersessionism.

emperor's favour – he would not attack the city – and protection: no one else would be allowed to attack it with impunity. There was a 'religious' dimension to this in that the cult of the emperor became part of the local cult and there were celebration – liturgies – to welcome the setting up of this relationship, imagined as the gospel's arrival, and on its anniversary. It was important to the city's inhabitants because, through it, they were conscious of the relationship to the emperor.[6] A gospel, and having a gospel, was shorthand for a treaty, a pact, and a statement of where the city stood in relationship to the larger world.

Within Second Temple Judaism a parallel notion of a treaty, but imagined in the now dated language of the Babylonians, was widely used: God had established a *covenant* with the people. The covenant had been made, remade, upheld, departed from, remade again, and was celebrated each day in the Temple in Jerusalem. The covenant – another word for this is 'testament' – was summed up in a phrase: 'And I will walk among you, and will be your God, and you shall be my people' (Lev 26:12) and is repeated in many other places.[7] God would bring the people into God's protection, the people would have no other God, and keep the Law which had been given them as their path.

Now, the followers of Jesus were taking the whole event of Jesus – not just his teaching but his life, death, and resurrection – and seeing this as just as decisive a moment in this covenant as the event of Moses receiving the Law on Sinai. Jesus was the new covenant, restoring the relationship. For many of the followers of Jesus, including Paul, the range of the covenant could be extended to those who were outside the historic bounds of Israel. It was, potentially, a covenant with all humanity. Indeed, this covenant was now being extended such that one could share directly in it without first becoming part of the covenant with Israel. One became, through Jesus, a member of the people of God, shared in its blessing, and became part of the final covenant community. Yet how does one communicate this notion of a covenant – established in Jesus and which meant accepting him, and not just accepting his teaching; seeing Jesus not simply as one more rabbi but as lord – to a Greek-speaking world? It was relatively easy to convey the notion of Jesus as one more religious teacher (the world was full of them) or as one more wise guide (philosophy was an after-dinner pastime) or even as wonder-worker/healer (there was no shortage of such people with very similar tales to those we find in the gospels), but the idea that one entered into a new, communal relationship with the all-holy God,

---

6. G.N. Stanton, *Jesus and Gospel* (Cambridge, 2004), pp. 25–35.
7. E.g. Jer 7:23 or 30:22, or Ezek 36:28.

Figure 6. A typical map from an old Bible.
We are often so familiar with such 'Bible maps' that we fail to examine
them. The most obvious implication of this map is that every travel
line starts and ends in a significant city. It witnesses that the Jesus
movement rapidly became an urban phenomenon – which mapped itself
almost exactly onto the existing urban phenomenon of Greek-speaking
Judaism in the Mediterranean basin.

through a relationship with this Jewish man and crucified criminal, was
virtually inexplicable. To those who were Jews, one could use all the
inherited language, imagery, myths, and the narratives of the scriptures
(what would later be called the Old Testament by Christians), but what
shorthand could you use with Greeks who were Gentiles?

Someone – before Paul began preaching because he used the term
as a familiar one – came up with the idea that Jesus was God's *gospel*
with this new human community. Just as the emperor sent a gospel to a
city-community where it was welcomed and honoured, so God had sent
a gospel to be accepted, honoured, and taken to heart – and this gospel
was a man: Jesus.[8] It might seem strange that we do not know the name
of the person who came up with the brilliant piece of transcultural

---

8. The word *euaggelion* is used in the Septuagint (e.g. at 2 Sam 4:10 or 18:22),
   but it does not appear to have influenced the choice of the word by these
   Greek-speaking followers of Jesus.

theological translation which identified 'the anointed one [the christ]' – a term meaningful to Jews – with 'the gospel' – a term meaningful to Gentiles – but it is just one more reminder of how little we know in detail about the early Jesus movement. It was an immediate success because Paul uses the word as if it is widely understood, a piece of common currency, which became central to his own identity: he is 'set apart for the gospel of God' (Rom 1:1). As is the way with the key words relating to the identity of any group, the word 'gospel' soon began to diffuse in meaning and take on new shades of significance as it covered more and more situations. In this process its primary meaning was smothered with baggage. So it moved from being what Jesus announced about God, to the fact of Jesus – he was 'the gospel', to telling the story about Jesus. Then the story teller became 'the evangelist' (gospeller), so then the story told by a gospeller became 'a gospel'; then it became one of the fixed set of stories called 'the gospels'. From that it became the name of a book, and.… But appreciating the original meaning of 'the gospel' is still at the heart of discipleship because that is what is common to those who have chosen to follow Jesus.

Appreciating that 'the gospel' is not a body of information or instructions, a communication, a philosophy, or something we can 'download' allows us to reread Paul and understand his concern for those Gentiles in Thessalonica. The repeated use by Paul of the word 'gospel' demonstrates a part of his concern: if they have listened to him, then they must accept the fact that they have entered a new relationship with God and one another. Now we can see how we need to reinterpret Paul when he says that 'our gospel came to you not in word only, but also in power and in the Holy Spirit and with full conviction' (1:5). Likewise, he is not engaged in teaching the gospel as if it were a course of instruction, but rather it is something declared: 'we had courage in our God to declare to you the gospel of God in spite of great opposition' (2:2) because 'just as we have been approved by God to be entrusted with the gospel, even so we speak, not to please mortals, but to please God who tests our hearts' (2:4). This new relationship with God changed the life of the people who accept it and this is why he 'so deeply [cares] for [them] that we [Paul, Silvanus and Timothy] are determined to share with you not only the gospel of God but also our own selves, because you have become very dear to us' (2:8). Witnessing to this fact of there being a gospel drives him and leads to his working lifestyle, so that he can remind them that 'you remember our labour and toil, brothers; we worked night and day, so that we might not burden any of you while we proclaimed to you the gospel of God' (2:9);

and that is why he 'sent Timothy, our brother and co-worker for God in proclaiming the gospel of Christ, to strengthen and encourage you for the sake of your faith' (3:2).

This group of Gentile Thessalonians have many questions and difficulties, but no matter what they must not forget that they are the beneficiaries of a gospel: that makes them into members of a community in God's special care. This awareness is basic to discipleship.

The Gospel of God

Two of the most startling differences between the churches in which Paul preached and later – and indeed modern – Christians are directly related to this question of the gospel and what it means. We have already touched on the first difference: seeing the gospel as a message, which is usually prefaced in modern preaching by some statement like 'the word "gospel" means "good news"', places the primacy on information – knowing about God, knowing a particular ethical code, or obtaining some sort of 'key' to life, meaning, or salvation. Yet the relationship that God offers humanity is not a trade-off: you will be saved if you have the key, but a gift and the proof of this is God's gospel: Jesus is with us.

The second difference is that later Christians were very conscious, based on seeing 'a gospel' as referring to a message or a collection of teaching, that they were preaching the gospel about Jesus. The gospel was his teaching and good news about Jesus. Paul emphasises that he proclaims the gospel of God. Put another way, Jesus' preaching was the good news about God, but later Christians' preaching put the emphasis the good news about Jesus. For Paul, Jesus is the gospel; for many Christians, Jesus is the source of the gospel. For the first generation to say that Jesus is the gospel is to make a statement about God's commitment to humanity, the proof of which is the crucified and risen Jesus. For later generations, Jesus is the teacher who told us that God loved us or else the one who persuaded God, by his death on the cross, to forgive us and love us. It is always interesting to ask this question: are you, as a Christian, primarily a witness to Jesus and his message about God; or, are you a witness to God and what the totality of Jesus's life and teaching tells us about God? This shift in focus – which later theologians would blur by suggesting that it makes little difference – is the source of a significant chasm in later generations' understanding of what they read in Paul's letters. For Paul, Jesus is a significant moment in the history of the Chosen People as they move towards the world's end. Within a few generations, Jesus would cease being seen by his followers as being part of Judaism and would be seen as the start of a whole new era in human history, the source of a new perfect religion, and the inheritance of Israel would be merely a preparation and a 'backstory'.

This move from Jesus' good news about God to the church's good news about Jesus can seem to be little more than an obscure point of interest only to academics. However, bear in mind the centuries of in-fighting among those who proclaim they are followers of Jesus about 'his' doctrine, doctrines about him, and the meaning of passages in Paul's letters. In these battles, academic and bloody, each side claims complete loyalty to the whole tradition or to the text – but this shift in our understanding of what we mean by 'the gospel' should cause everyone to pause and note the differences in the ways we remember and the ways we tell our stories. The salient memory is always shifting,[9] and this should lead us to behave with far more circumspection with our claims to knowing what 'the Christian doctrine' is. This was put another way by Johann Baptist Metz: 'Christianity is not really a community that interprets and gives arguments, but rather a community that remembers and tells stories.'[10]

Where are we in Time

Paul, responding to this Gentile church of Jesus-followers in Thessalonica, found himself having to develop his own understanding of what was involved in discipleship. We see this in the way he dealt with questions about when the great 'day of the Lord' would come (1 Thess 5:1). This was the time, mentioned by the prophets and probably mentioned by Jesus, in the future when God would intervene

---

9. The notion of 'salient memory', the focus of our memory and how it relates to our understanding, the significance of a memory at a particular time, has been explored by B. Schwartz, 'Memory as a Cultural System: Abraham Lincoln in World War II', *American Sociological Review*, 61 (1996), pp. 908–27, and related to early Christian memories of Jesus by him in Schwartz, 'Christian Origins: Historical Truth and Social Memory', in A. Kirk and T. Thatcher (eds.), *Tradition and Text: Uses of the Past in Early Christianity* (Atlanta, GA, 2005), pp. 43–56.

10. J.B. Metz, *Faith in History and Society: Toward a Practical Fundamental Theology*, ed. and tr. J.M. Ashely (New York, 2007), p. 194.

and bring the whole creation to completion and judgement. At the time that he wrote the letter Paul imagined this 'day' as coming in the very near future, indeed in his own lifetime. The group he is writing to are clearly concerned about what was going to happen to members of their community who had already died and presumably their question was 'since X and Y have now died and did not live long enough to see this great day of the Lord's coming [by which they meant the intervention of God rather than a second coming of the Christ], had they lost out on all the promises?' Paul replies: 'If we believe that Jesus died and rose again, then so also we believe God will bring with him [to heavenly perfection] those who have fallen asleep as Christians' (4:14). And then he shows that he imagines this taking place in his own lifetime:

> For this we declare to you by the word of the Lord, that we who are alive, who are left until the coming of the Lord, will surely not go ahead of those who have died. For the Lord himself, with a cry of command, with the archangel's call and with the sound of God's trumpet, will descend from heaven, and the dead in Christ will rise first. Then we who are alive, who are left, will be caught up (*harpagésometha*) in the clouds together with them to meet the Lord in the air; and so we will be with the Lord forever. Therefore encourage one another with these words (4:15–18).

It is very hard for any modern Christian – knowing that what Paul was expecting and waiting for did not happen – to imagine their way back into this view of the world. But one major element of that vision was that Paul not only saw himself within years of 'the end' but also imagined Jesus not as the beginning of something new, a new start or the founder of a new religion, but as a conclusion. Jesus' life, death, and resurrection ushered in the final act. Paul lived in a world grown old, not in a 'start-up'. They – Paul and the community for whom he is writing – are at the end of history, there is no long future stretching out in front of them for which they should be laying foundations, and their concern is why the final act seems to have been delayed by months or, at most, by a couple of years. Having this perspective makes them hear Paul's words in a wholly different way to how most of us hear them.

It is worth pausing to consider the questions that these few short verses, written probably without a great deal of deliberation to fend off questions troubling a few people at one moment, throw up for Christians today. First, when read with solemnity – whether in a liturgical assembly or in a Bible-study group – it is all too easy to imagine that every utterance like this is an oracle: words endowed with a truth that transcends our fractured historical moments. Yet here we see Paul acting as a theologian – seeking to make sense of facts and beliefs by aligning them the best way he can at the moment. This is not simply 'thinking on the hoof' but nor is it carefully weighed judgements intended to be treated as 'written in stone'. It is a response to a situation that would encourage those who were troubled by the question. Secondly, within some strands of Protestantism in the United States these verses have taken on a life of their own and a whole vision of 'the end times' (coming soon) has been built up upon them. Reading 4:17 as detailed description of the moment of the end of time, some people have built a whole scenario called 'the rapture'[11] and are happy to speak of this as a future event within the same frames of reference they might speak of 'when the snow comes next winter'. While apocalypticism has been a more or less constant element in Christianity, this notion takes the idea that there are secrets about the future hidden in sacred books to a whole new level. The basic idea (for most who adhere to it) is that the world is going to be subjected to a seven-year 'tribulation' but that God will rescue his own before this happens by snatching them up into the air to be with him. It is a future fantasy that, though the sinners will soon be given their just punishments, the chosen ones will be picked out beforehand in the sudden miraculous moment of 'the rapture'. Such notions should serve as a reminder that when we imagine our religious mythic language – what we use to make sense of what is beyond the world of things and even language – describing the functioning of the world around us, we are confusing ourselves, generating nonsense, and betraying the mystery we seek. The fact that Paul, at one moment in his life, was similarly mired in such confusion cannot be viewed as its justification. Thirdly, when we read this passage, we silently mutate its meaning from the immediate future to being a metaphor for a time beyond time. Such a shift in perspective may seem drastic in that we are not reading what Paul said but what makes sense to

---

[11.] The term is derived from Paul's use of *harpagésometha,* which can be rendered in various ways such as 'we will be caught up' (the most common English translation) or 'snatched up' – often with the addition of 'suddenly' to grasp the sense of a quick and forceful action – and it was this future event that has been named 'the rapture' since the mid-nineteenth century. My own favoured rendering is 'we will be plucked out' – but the more the translation reflects the vigour of Paul's language, the more distracting it can be.

us, but is that anything more than a more explicit instance of what we are doing every time we read these ancient texts and seek from them light for our path? We make sense of Paul by misrepresenting him in answer to our questions, just as he made sense of his questions by misrepresenting the relationship between God as the end-point of the creation and the material world around him. Every decoding is another encoding.

Paul Seeking Answers and a Way Forward within a Community

For most of Christian history there has been a practice of turning to the Bible as a place for finding answers and 'what the Bible teaches', and of seeking to settle arguments with quotations from Paul that 'clinch the argument'. Yet, as Metz noted, 'Christianity is not really a community that interprets and gives arguments' and finding the path of discipleship for an individual in a community involves investigating and reflecting and speculating and telling stories: it is far harder than simply looking up a book. In 1 Thessalonians we see Paul engaged in this process, trying to draw together his faith in the God of Israel, bear witness to what he believes is the significance of the event of Jesus, support a community by his teaching, and figure out a discrepancy between religious expectation about 'the day of the Lord' and the actual facts. He tries to put it all together and makes a mess of it. The answer of the moment was not one that stood the test of time.

When Paul realised this we do not know – but he never returned to the theme nor the imagery, and it never gained traction among other teachers in the early churches – and it is possible that almost on uttering his answer, he began to think through a better solution. A couple of verses later he is hesitant about saying anything 'about times and seasons' (5:1)[12] as if responding to the question: will the End come at

---

[12.] We have to be careful about using phrases such as 'in the next chapter' because we are apt to forget that these chapter divisions were a product of the twelfth century – and reflect how they read Paul – and that there were many other division systems used before then in the history of Christianity. See D. De Bruyne, *Summaries, Divisions and Rubrics of the Latin Bible* (Turnhout, 2014) for the alternatives. In terms of Paul's thinking, the letter appears to have 4:13–5:4 as a 'unit' dealing with questions about when the Day of the Lord would come.

a particular festival over the course of their liturgical year?[13] However, we are the richer for being able to observe Paul in the process of seeking answers to real questions.

Paul, likewise, does not want to become distracted with the detailed questions that were disturbing some in the group: there is a bigger concern which is living as sons and daughters of the light. It is this concentration on the positive attitudes that a community of disciples should adopt that is his real answer to questions about the end – whatever happens, keep growing as followers. The practical now has priority over theological speculations. This consists in living responsible lives wearing faith and love as a cuirass and having confidence in being saved as a helmet (5:8). This is contrary to a constant human tendency to imagine that fate, or the god, or God is intent on our destruction: 'because God has not set as our destiny his anger, but to obtain safely though our Lord Jesus Christ' (5:9). Jesus is our gospel of God's loving intentions.

It is this hope that is the basis of the behaviour of the group towards one another. This leads Paul to quote a string of slogans that had probably been forged in catchphrases through repetition in preaching. The group – all the commands are in the plural – should keep to this plan of action:

> *Rejoice ye always.*
> *Pray ye without ceasing.*
> *Give ye thanks in all circumstances ...*
> *Quench ye not the Spirit.*
> *Despise ye not the words of prophets ...*
> *Hold ye fast to what is good.*
> *Abstain ye from every form of evil. (5:16–22)*

Taken in their totality this is a recipe for a community that could imagine itself as 'the sons [and daughters] of the light and the day'. If all the energy that has been generated over the centuries by what this letter tells us about the end of time and what God might do in those final moments had been committed to making these the slogans of Christianity, the world might now be a very different place. Just imagine if 'Rejoice always!' was as familiar a Christian sentiment as 'Fear the Lord!'

[13.] The early communities continued with their liturgical year as Jews – note Paul in 1 Cor 16:8 observing Pentecost/Shavuot – and this became the remembering structure into which Gentiles were drawn.

Chapter 4

Disciples, Disputes, and Factions – and Reconciliation Structures

In the last chapter we had some very early glimpses of an actual community of disciples, the Graeco-Roman non-Jewish followers of Jesus in Thessalonica who were troubled by the discrepancies between what they had been taught by such teachers as Paul, Silvanus, Timothy, and others, and what they were actually experiencing. They imagined the end of the universe, the completion of history, was at hand, but still their fellow disciples were dying and there was no sign of an imminent divine intervention. This might seem to be a good point to discuss the values of such a community, the nature of their life as a community, and how they would like to be recognised as belonging within a church. Drawing a picture of such a community, in the springtime of faith, is both attractive and, apparently, useful for modern disciples.

There is, moreover, excellent precedent for such a layout of topics. Luke, writing sometime in the first half of the second century in the Acts of the Apostles, takes the very first opportunity he has to give a description of how wonderful the community life was and its cohesion and harmony. Luke wants his audience to know that it all started well. Having described the events and preaching of Peter that took place on the festival of Pentecost following the ascension of Jesus, Luke writes:

> So those who received his word were baptised, and there were added that day about three thousand souls. And they devoted themselves to the apostles' teaching and fellowship, to the breaking of the loaf and the prayers. And fear came upon

every soul; and many wonders and signs were done through the apostles. And all who believed were together and had all things in common; and they sold their possessions and goods and distributed them to all, as any had need. And day by day, attending the temple together and breaking the loaf in their homes, they partook of food with glad and generous hearts, praising God and having favour with all the people. And the Lord added to their number day by day those who were being saved. (2:41–47)

This little vignette, labelled in many Bibles as 'life among the believers', is presented as both a fact and a norm, and the implicit lesson is: get back to that perfection!

However, when we examine what we know about those early communities the picture that emerges is more complicated. We see that the communities were far less harmonious, that factions and disputes were common, and that the glowing image of fraternal sharing was created as an ideal for imitation in the face of far less attractive facts on the ground. Meanwhile, we see that the communities were seeking out reconciliation structures that might allay the fissiparous tendencies that were hurting them just as they beset every human grouping.

Is there another way to arrange topics relating to discipleship? I believe that beginning with the actual problems has much to recommend it. It allows us to grasp the need for reconciliation as a basis of discipleship far more effectively than using a mythic ideal of original harmony. With the mythic starting point, there is always a quest for the source of the disease – be it heresy, bad practices, or wilful contrariness – and a blame-game: who is the bad person who has disrupted our happiness? If we assume that imperfect, incomplete, and fallible human beings, even when seeking God with the Spirit dwelling within their hearts, generate difficulties for one another and can cause bitter disputes to arise, this allows us to have a far more realistic grasp of our situation. Moreover, it makes us view reconciliation as a basic ongoing challenge of living together, rather than as a patch-up, an afterthought, or a compromise. It also removes another systemic weakness of beginning with 'what we believe should be the case' as if it were a fact: we are not tempted to see reconciliation (and its inevitable compromises) as moral weakness or a dilution of Christian purity. 'Compromise' in that scenario is a dirty word smacking of treason! But compromise is not a dirty word nor a mark of weakness or lack of zeal. Compromise recognises the complexity of our situation and is part of loving each other and seeking the good – given that no one is perfect or infallible. Indeed, this fear of 'going soft on sin' – by acknowledging the incompleteness of our actual reality – has been a recurrent problem in the experience of all the churches, and, in itself, has produced more alienation, often deepening divisions into unbridgeable chasms.

In short, starting with 'a golden age' is both historically fraudulent (it was not so) and theologically misleading (we cannot construct a perfect 'now'). This is because the Christian task is not to get back to a pristine past – that was the pagan vision of history where a 'golden age' decayed to a 'silver age' and that has now degenerated to our present rusty condition – but to move forward toward the Kingdom when the Christ will be all in all (1 Cor 15:28).[1] Believers in the God of Israel look forwards. There was never a perfect church in the past, nor is there an ideal church against which actual experience can be measured: there is just the reality of what we are, our consciousness that we can do better, and the need to grow in wisdom and holiness. To be a disciple, and the discipleship of a church, is a work in progress.

A World of Factions

But how fractured were the early communities? The answer to this does not come in the form a clear narrative: we have no document called 'a list of our grievances'. But when we assemble the information from occasional references in our sources, from inferences about their concerns with community reconciliation, and from the structures they put in place – such as the safeguards mentioned in the *Didache* regarding pseudo-prophets[2] – a picture emerges that shows that the halcyon, idyllic, 'apostolic' period so often appealed to in popular images of 'the early church' is mythic (albeit a myth abetted by such writers as Luke in the Acts of the Apostles).

Before looking at some of the practical disputes about what should happen in the groups, we should also note that there was no moment of perfect, unified belief – there never was an original 'orthodoxy' to which we might 'return'. That there were disputes about even what would later be seen as central elements of Christian belief is nowhere better

---

[1.] There is perhaps no better example of this 'looking to the future' dimension of Jewish thinking from the documents from the first-century followers of Jesus than 1 Cor 15:12–58.

[2.] See A. Milavec, 'Distinguishing True and False Prophets: The Protective Wisdom of the *Didache*', *Journal of Early Christian Studies,* 2 (1994), 117–36.

exemplified than in Paul's concerns, seen in 1 Corinthians 15, that all followers of Jesus should both believe in his resurrection and see the fact of Jesus' resurrection as of importance to them in their discipleship.

Some of the most frequently quoted passages from the canonical collection come from 1 Corinthians 15: it offers us a series of brilliant images – 'for the trumpet will sound, and the dead shall be raised imperishable, and we shall be changed' (v. 52) – that form a central element in our celebrations at Easter, at funerals, and they echo in our heads from hearing Handel's *Messiah*. However, what is far less commented upon is that Paul is so anxious to write about the resurrection because for some in Corinth it was not considered important. Paul justifies making his argument because 'some of you say that there is no resurrection of the dead' (v. 12). Why would the community there, made up of Jews and Gentiles, say this? We simply do not know the facts with any certainty. The probable answer has several elements. First, belief in the notion of a 'resurrection' was not universal among Jews. Some did see resurrection as part of the promised future of the Righteous, others did not – a difference in theology that was remembered by Luke and referred to in Acts 23:6–8. So, a difference among Jewish followers of Jesus is quite likely: some may have been more fascinated by Jesus's teaching and approach to practice, and it is easy to imagine them arguing with those who concentrated on the significance of Jesus being put to death as a cosmic event. Second, the notion of resurrection – that there would be anything bodily after death – was repugnant to Greek culture. Greek culture saw death as an immortal soul being liberated from the limitations of the body and the impurity of the material. Allowing the soul to be free was a good thing: it was a spirit which had been trapped in the body, and so the idea of further imprisonment in a resurrected body (literally: 'a body-that-had-stood-up-again') was repulsive. The teaching of Jesus might be appealing, and the practices of the community attractive, but *post-mortem* imprisonment in a body was not acceptable. This cultural suspicion regarding the body would long survive Paul, and become part of the background noise in Christian spirituality down to our own day.[3] The interesting point here is that Paul does not use belief in resurrection as a criterion of belonging in the way that later church groups would have doctrinal tick-boxes. The community is the community, and if some have what Paul considers wayward beliefs, he seeks to correct them. For Paul, disciples have joined a community rather than signed up to a theological manifesto.

[3.] N. Loudovikos, *Analogical Identities: The Creation of the Christian Self – Beyond Spirituality and Mysticism in the Patristic Era* (Turnhout, 2019).

However, there were far more practical issues which were dividing the churches than questions about resurrection. The fact that Paul has to present himself as one who earns his own keep, rather than being supported by the churches in which he teaches, points to disputes about money. From the *Didache* we learn that there were those who were sponging off communities in the name of being teachers. Consequently, rules had to be put in place to distinguish between true and false prophets – a false prophet is not one whose witness is considered doctrinally suspect but one whose behaviour is that of a con-artist. They even had a disparaging term for all these wandering peddlers of teaching, 'christhawkers' (*christemporoi*), who were really only trying to line their pockets or their bellies in the name of preaching the gospel.[4]

Figure 7. Christianity as a brand: a shop window in Italy.
Seeing Christianity as a brand – and as a consumer commodity –
is neither a new activity nor one confined to the margins. In the first
century there were those the *Didache* refers to as 'christhawkers'; today
we have those who present discipleship as the key to success in life
('The Prosperity Gospel') or a quick, self-help way to happiness.

---

4. *Didache* 12:5.

Even within communities, the demands of seeing each other as brothers and sisters, as equals, because 'God does not show partiality' (Rom 2:11),[5] was too much. While it was most pleasant to eat with one's friends, it was quite another to have to share a table with 'others'. Jews did not like sharing with Gentiles because of ritual purity at meals – and sharing a table with women was always problematic. Gentiles might object to being lumped side by side with Jews. In a stratified society, many wanted client relationships to trump notions of equality, and then there is a problem of slaves. Would a slave who is a fellow diner as a disciple get ideas about her/his station afterwards? When we read Paul's wonderful encomium on the divine welcome in 1 Corinthians 1:4–9, we often skip over why he had to write it, which is made clear immediately afterwards in his awareness of problems in Corinth (1 Cor 1:10–13).

It is interesting to read these two paragraphs in parallel:

I give thanks to God always for you all,	I appeal to all of you, brothers,
because of the grace of God	by the name of our lord, Jesus,
which was given to you all in Jesus,	the anointed one,
the anointed one,	that you all agree
that in every way,	and that there be no dissentions among you,
you all were enriched in him	rather,
with all speech	that you be united in the same mind,
and all knowledge	and the same judgement.
– even as the testimony to the Christ	My brothers,
was confirmed among you	I have been told … that there is quarrelling among you.
so that you are not lacking in any spiritual gift,	

---

5. This phrase 'God does not show partiality' was one of Paul's slogans: he used in in Rom 2:11 and Gal 2:6 – and it is directly echoed in Acts 2:6 and 10:34. The phrase also has echoes in other writings of the churches: Col 3:25; Eph 6:9 (see A. Standhartinger, 'The Origin and Intention of the Household Code in the Letter to the Colossians', *Journal for the Study of the New Testament*, 79 (2000), p. 129); Jas 2:1 and 1 Pet 1:17 – the repetitions show how problematic the idea was.

as you wait for the revealing of our lord, Jesus, the Christ	What I refer to is this:
who will sustain you to the end	One says 'I belong to Paul'
	Another 'I belong to Apollos'
guiltless in the day of our lord Jesus,	Another 'I belong to Christ'
the Christ.	Is the Christ divided?
God is faithful,	
who called you all into the community of his Son,	
Jesus, the Christ, our lord	
1 Cor 1:4–9	1 Cor 1:10–13

We shall examine in this book's next chapter some very specific sources of division in the churches and the way they conducted their gatherings, but for now it is sufficient to make this point: if there had been fewer disagreements and squabbles in the early churches, then we would probably now have a much smaller collection of Pauline letters. In every one of the genuine letters, we have problems just below the surface: the letters are Paul's attempts to move communities beyond the limitations of vision exposed in disputes. So, when we hear him preach his great embracing vision:

For as many of you as were baptised into Christ
have put on Christ.
There is neither Jew nor Greek
there is neither slave nor free,
there is neither male nor female,
for you are all one in Christ Jesus (Gal 3:27–8)

we have to think 'backwards'. The reason Paul so exhorts them is that these were the very distinctions that the churches were insisting upon. Jews did not want to mix with Gentiles: they certainly did not want to eat at the same table as them – and the same went for eating with women who were not family members. Gentile men might not have the same worries about ritual purity as the Jews that were now their 'brothers' and 'sisters', but it was best for everyone if there was some decorum: so let the men eat together and the women eat together – and probably the women were as insistent on this among themselves as the men.[6] And as for the slaves: while obviously a slave might want to eat with her/his master; one did have to acknowledge reality and that meant that, while they might be one in the Christ, they were anything but one in every other way. Indeed, in all our early documents, praises of the need for unity are an index of the extent of actual division.

The actual challenges of discipleship that these social divisions show us are not those we usually imagine. However, it is precisely these kinds of challenge that are so difficult for us Christians of the twenty-first century. We might enjoy the sense of belonging to our particular church, we might be smug in our own social milieu, but seeking an ever-expanding human fraternity is something we 'park' on the level of nice theory. If we do take this notion seriously, then with it goes a commitment to human equality in human opportunity and not just 'before God'. This is even more socially demanding than asking someone in a purity conscious society to share food with someone impure. To be willing to address other disciples as 'sister' and 'brother' can seem just the in-house jargon of my group – and even then it sounds a bit corny – but it becomes a real issue about life and living if we consider that it means we have to be conscious of human slavery, exploitation of workers, and neo-colonialism. Then it is as difficult as a master sharing a table with his slave while listening to a story about his Teacher who says that he was among those at table as 'one who serves'. Hearing the whole sentence could be rather irritating to a slave-owning Christian: 'For who is greater, one who sits at the table, or one who serves? Is it not he who sits at the table? But I am among you as one who serves' (Luke 22:27).

Discipleship seems to involve finding ourselves irritated by the clash of our attitudes with the implications of those we claim to espouse. Confronting this is more awkward than setting out a 'things to do' list of pious actions.

---

6. Although the comments of B.J. Bauman-Martin, 'Women on the Edge: New Perspectives on Women in the Petrine *Haustafel*', *Journal of Biblical Literature,* 123 (2004), pp. 253–79, relate directly to a later period (i.e. the early second century when the letter we call '1 Peter' was composed), they are applicable more generally to the cultural situation of the early churches of Paul's time.

How do we Read Luke's Presentations of Harmony?

If we can see disputes at every turn in not only Paul's letters, but in community guidelines such as the *Didache*, the 'household codes' found in other documents,[7] simmering in the background – the life-situation – of the gospels, as well as in other texts such as the letter from a Roman church to a Corinthian church known as '1 Clement', what are we to make of the very different picture that we get from reading the Acts of the Apostles?

At the outset, let us note that for most of the period between the late second century and the later nineteenth century the canonical text known as Acts has been seen as a direct factual account of what happened in the churches – presented collectively as 'the Christians' on the basis of Acts 11:26 – until Paul's arrival in Rome for his trial. This historical reading is still prevalent, as a default, in many Christian groups today: they appeal to what Luke *says* as simply an account of what *happened*. Second, we should note that there is no simple way to reconcile what we see in other documents with what we find in Acts: there are real contradictions, not merely differences of understanding that can be harmonised through ingenious scholarship. This creates tensions in churches because some have so committed themselves to the notion of a perfect original era that they can use simply as a prototype that they recoil at the notion that Luke's picture is 'fancy' rather than 'fact'. Other groups are so committed to the notion of the biblical texts as 'the inspired word' of God that pointing to historical ineptitude of Luke seems little less than treason. Third, popes, patriarchs, and pastors when faced with the less than lovely face of Christianity today often engage in a little bit of off-the-cuff Platonism and invite us to contemplate an ideal Church – and flesh it out with quotes from Acts – rather than facing the actual situation that the messy mob we Christians are is the only church that exists.

There is no ideal church – just the one we have.

I am fairly sure that Luke did not set out to deceive later generations but that he played a rhetorical game with his audience that would have been familiar to most authors – Jewish, Christian, or other – of

---

7. There are short texts which deal with how a household – women, children, slaves – should be ruled by someone who wants to consider himself a Christian. The fact that we have repetitions of them (Col 3:18–4:1; Eph 5:21–6:9; Tit 2:1–10; and 1 Pet 2:18–3:7) suggests that some Christians did not think the usual rules of their society should apply – and the response was this restatement of traditional paternal authority. See A. Standhartinger, 'The Origin and Intention of the Household Code in the Letter to the Colossians'.

his time. Luke – in both his gospel and Acts – is an evangelist not an historian in any sense of the word that we would recognise. Let us speculate as to what his starting question was: how does one convince these churches that they are falling short in their discipleship without haranguing them, making them close their ears, and alienating them? One strategy is to imagine a perfect group and then let the audience measure themselves against it. Such ideal societies can be found in Greek pagan writers (e.g. Plato in the *Republic* or the *Timaeus*), in Jewish writings from the times before Luke (such as the Books of Tobit and Judith), which use the imagery of a past time or a foreign situation a critique-cum-sermon for their author's time. Luke does likewise and paints the first generation of disciples as the group who did it well; and then he lets his audience assess for themselves how they have fallen away. Luke's method is rhetorical – and dangerous. It is dangerous because we – not the intended audience – can see it as a golden moment rather than as a perpetual challenge.

We have a Dream

Surprisingly, once we have moved away from the notion of Acts as history, its potential as guide for a community of disciples today is suddenly released. Acts functions for us in a manner equivalent to Martin Luther King's 'I have a dream' speech in that it holds before us the community values that we should be striving towards now as our future. The paradox is that Acts is more about the wondrous Christian future than a golden Christian past.

If we want to see what this dream looks like we can just pick on any of the themes that run through Acts. For example, an aspect of discipleship that Acts presents to us is the significance of a commitment to ecumenism. This is often simply a concern of church leaders where it is part of their diplomacy, but Acts presents us with a whole network of churches, seeking to work harmoniously in the greater task of taking the message from Jerusalem, to Judaea and Samaria, and out to the ends of the earth (Acts 1:8) – or, at least, the cities of Luke's Greek world. Luke invites the groups to stop looking at their own situations and dream of the big, global picture.[8] Is this

---

[8.] T. O'Loughlin, 'Sharing Food and Breaking Boundaries: Reading of Acts 10–11:18 as a Key to Luke's Ecumenical Agenda in Acts', *Transformation*, 32 (2015), pp. 27–37.

an aspect of discipleship you recognise? Many churches view their own network as equivalent to the whole. Many see real engagement with differing churches as diminution or contamination. But the fact of division is real and, therefore, making bridges is part of the work of everyone who can see that the Kingdom is bigger than their particular locality.

The churches that Luke visited were stressed groups divided along ethnic, social, and party lines. That some were for Apollos and some for Paul (1 Cor 3:4) tells us far more than the names of two early apostles. Likewise, how each community was to relate to the larger society – such as whether one could eat meat that had been part of the normal civic system of sacrifices – were live sources of bitterness. No doubt one side saw their stance as virtue signalling, while the other side saw the matters regarding purity/syncretism as no more than religious obscurantism. In this situation Luke dreams of moments of reconciliation following discussion, prayer, and a mutual quest for enlightenment. What later ecclesiastics saw as 'the Council of Jerusalem' was a picture of an ideal pattern for overcoming divisions and promoting reconciliation. This too is a part of discipleship; promoting reconciliation between factions before they lead to breakdown, bitterness, and the wasteful false-witness of division. While many churches speak about reconciliation in the context of discipleship – for example, Roman Catholics now refer to 'the Sacrament of Reconciliation' as the formal means of seeking forgiveness for sins committed after baptism – this often is interpreted in a very narrow, individualistic sense. Reconciliation is thought about in terms of an individual sinner being reconciled with God, but reconciliation is a much larger theme than this private 'clearing of accounts'. The Lukan dream is far more embracing: he imagines seeking out reconciliation within communities and between communities as the work to which his listeners should dedicate themselves. To be a disciple means to be someone who not only seeks to avert being disruptive – a 'thou shalt not' – but who promotes reconciliation in the midst of discord – a 'thou shalt'. Reconciliation is a community need rather than a private matter, and it is basic to what disciples have to offer because, when it comes to human strife, 'if you are not part of the solution, you are part of the problem'.

We might generalise this theologically: if God in the Christ was reconciling the world to himself (2 Cor 5:19), then the followers of the Christ are called to be agents of reconciliation, as well as messengers of reconciliation, in their lives, their communities, and in the world.

Structures

We are now in a position to locate some of the practices that are found in Christian communities which can be seen as exploring this notion of overcoming ruptures between people. The most obvious is the 'the peace' or 'the sign of peace' that many churches have as part of the eucharistic liturgies. For some this is just a bit of user-friendly ritual intended to 'humanise' liturgy. For others, it is a moment to be avoided: a confusion of human communion with divine communion which distracts. For many, it is just tokenism: pretending that I wish someone I hardly know 'peace' as a 'sister' or a 'brother', when we will both return to a confrontational anonymity the moment the service ends. While such negative reactions are 'the facts on the ground', they also reveal just how hard it is to embed being a conciliator within our lives.

Figure 8. A Confession Box.
Reconciliation cannot be reduced to formulae. Perhaps the greatest instance of such a reduction has been the rise of individual rituals such as the 'Confession' – officially referred to by Roman Catholics as 'the sacrament of reconciliation' – where the notion of private account with God trumps the challenge of practicing reconciliation as part of a life of discipleship.

However, if we view our formal ritual actions as our dreams of what our discipleship should be – in a parallel way to how we should read Acts – then we might appreciate this gesture as a prayer for a better world. The gesture – reaching out to someone we may not know – and being willing to exchange touch and word expresses a common commitment among we who have gathered. It is an expression of the reconciliation theme within the Lord's Prayer: 'forgive us our trespasses *as* we forgive those who trespass against us'.

Reconciliation is not merely a religious attitude, or being willing 'to forgive and forget', but makes deeper demands. We live within human webs of connections, societies, and we know just how easily these can foster disruption and division. Disciples can find themselves in situations of condoning such behaviour. Here are two situations which might illustrate just how much attention and dedication is called for. The first case is seemingly very simple: there is a shortage of nurses and medical doctors in many developed countries. Meanwhile, in poorer countries there are many willing to train and qualify in these fields – and who would like to migrate for economic reasons to the developed world. This, at first sight, is a matter of supply and demand in skills, and to involve moral questions only accidentally (e.g. they should get fair wages when they arrive) if at all. Then, if a wealthy state's government facilitates and encourages this, it is no more than facilitating an economic transaction that benefits its people, and all concerned (the health system and its new migrant workers) are happy. But if we think of this in terms of the inequalities between states and living conditions, and the notion that one group can live off another group by stripping it of its assets, and skilled people are a community's greatest asset, then the situation is changed. Looked at as one society viewing another simply as 'raw material' – an ever-present source of human evil – then it is eminently a moral issue. One society, in greater need of medical skills than one's own, is being deliberately stripped of them and the wants of one's own country given an absolute and superior status. This is a disruption that causes suffering, and merely claiming to reject such colonialism is not enough: seeking human reconciliation means that such processes should be rejected. But we should not imagine that seeing these needs for reconciliation is an easy matter – for example, the Roman Catholic Church in the developed world, faced with diminishing pool of full-time, celibate ministers, is increasingly 'importing' clergy from Africa, India, and the South-East Asian countries. This is done without reference to the relative available of clergy in the developed and undeveloped countries, nor without reference to the best use of scarce educational resources in developing countries. While this is rationalised as 'an example of [that church's] catholicity' and even presented as somehow a worthwhile activity, it is, in fact, colonialism: the 'outpost' is serving the metropolis. Here is an action – justified in terms of 'discipleship' – that is actually running counter to the real needs of the churches.

The second situation is even more toxic in that it can lead to direct violence towards others. Is there an easier way to make people come together, and stick together, than to give them a common enemy, and portray some nearby group as 'other', wicked, dangerous, and a threat not only to your way of life, your culture, but your very survival? Any leader – such as a politician wrapping himself in a flag and inciting nationalism – who can convince a people that they are in such a danger will be sure of a following. Recent human history is littered with the suffering caused by such appeals to nationalism (perhaps the most dangerous form of sectionalism and secular sectarianism) as a means of binding a group together. While collective rivalry adds zest in sport – *our* team against *their* team – and provides an occasion for bonding rituals within a society, when this is extended to the actual treatment of other societies it is an ethical question for Christians, because we have this vision of God's peace spreading out, through disciples, to the ends of the earth. One cannot adopt being a reconciler/disciple as part of one's identity before God and then condone policies that work to create barriers and deadly rivalries between peoples.

Reconciliation is hard enough when it means shaking hands and agreeing to a fresh start after a quarrel because deep inside each of us there is the desire to have won and our memory can rake over the coals for us to reignite the dispute. When it comes to being part of Christian identity and witness it is all the more difficult. That Luke saw the chasm between the vision of what should be 'the Christian thing' and the reality of the divisions in the churches he visited was his real historical insight.

Chapter 5

Amazing Grace

Moving Onwards as Wounded Pilgrims

In the last chapter we saw how the early communities were far from the ideal groups of popular Christian memory and concluded by noting that the difficulties of discipleship might be more profound than we often want to acknowledge. Does this mean that discipleship is an ideal that we intellectually espouse, but which has little concrete reality in our day-to-day lives? Perhaps discipleship is only for the few – the spiritual top athletes – while for the rest of us it is to be admired from afar but we have to be content with a simpler set of rules as the best we can manage? Perhaps we should abandon the larger vision as just the realm of 'theory' and concentrate on ourselves as individuals, and imagine the demands of being a follower in terms of a personal tally sheet with God? All three of these approaches to discipleship have been pressed into use by Christians down the centuries. Similarly, each has been rejected down the centuries by other Christians as a betrayal of the gospel proclaimed by Jesus. Hence, any discussion of discipleship needs to examine them before a search for a better model can be undertaken.

Christianity is an Ideal

There is a long history of idealism within Christianity, not least because so much of our theology has been produced by writers – both Greek and Latin – who have been enthralled by Plato and various forms of

Figure 9. A study in inequality.
Church architecture can reveal the ecclesiology of ministers.
This community claims that their eucharistic activity is 'the centre and summit' of their existence, but there are clearly the 'big people' who are at the table, and many 'little people' who watch on from the stalls.

Neoplatonic thought. But the kernel of all such idealism is that the actual life we live as human beings is but a reflection of a more real existence that is awaiting us. We, the argument goes, are either trapped in the noise, friction, or limitations of matter, and long for release; or else we should view this life as no more than a painful antechamber to 'real' reality when freed from limits, distraction, impurity we can be 'as we should be'. It is an approach which is often more focussed on death than on life and living life. This approach that we should be angels but are spancelled by our bodies and materiality is further complicated in that one can easily find any number of quotations from the New Testament that can be read in terms of this 'spirit' versus 'matter' approach. Typical is this sentence from Paul:

> For the desires of the flesh are against the Spirit, and the desires of the Spirit are against the flesh; for these are opposed to each other, to prevent you from doing what you would. (Gal 5:17)

While such oppositional thinking is a basic human way of making any point with clarity – and spirit/matter is a convenient opposition and appears in virtually all human discourse – should we see this as an endorsement of idealism?

A basic weakness of the approach is that it assumes that discipleship is actually impossible and that the whole system is set up so that in our everyday lives we will fail. Could this be seen as the will of a god whom we declare to be the truth, to be our creator, and in whom we can trust? Idealism, in presenting us with a situation which is impossible, undermines the notion that we have an insight into the loving plan of the Creator for humankind. A further weakness of the approach is that it assumes that the real focus of discipleship is not here – in the actual world in which we are living and in which we hear the call to 'come, follow me' – but in some other world (be that a future ideal realm or some 'higher' state in a cycle of reincarnations). Yet it is here as limited and very complex human animals that we set out on the path! For Christians, the fundamental flaw with idealisms – even when they are espoused as a philosophical system – is that we confess that God has come among us, pitched his tent in our midst (John 1:14), in Jesus of Nazareth. What we claim to know about God's love is what we see in another human being. It is that fellow human, Jesus, who calls us to discipleship. However we decide to imagine the human situation and the call to take a pathway towards God, that pathway may require us to dream of a far better world than this one right now, but it must be a really possible world where humans can live.

A Two-Tier Christianity

Another way of configuring the call to holiness is to imagine humanity made up of two classes. First, there are the ordinary folk who find it all too much, given that they have to work for a living, are married with families, and have to cope with all the day-to-day demands that weigh them down, and limit their freedom. The demands of prayer, lifestyle, reflection, dedication may all seem lovely – and very worthy in themselves – but they have enough to be doing just to survive, and, that done, if they still have any time they grasp whatever brief moment of happiness presents itself. Second, there are those who have separated themselves from 'the world' and from all those distracting concerns, and who really focus on discipleship. For this group, discipleship has become a profession – and they claim that it is not only equivalent to a full-time job but requires celibacy and living apart from others. As with idealism, this is a very human way of constructing a religion: monasticism in various forms can be found in many religions. It was to be found among the Qumran community within Judaism at the time of Jesus, it can be found many strands of Buddhism (arguably the religion most consistent with the basic tenets of monasticism), and, of course, the history of Christianity cannot be understood without taking into account that monasticism was so pervasive that it came to be identified as the powerhouse of faith for many people. In this view there are two distinct standards to follow: 'the way of perfection' – often linked to 'the evangelical counsels' of poverty, celibacy, and obedience – and 'the way of the world' which is based on avoiding sin – especially as set out in the 'the ten commandments' – and some 'good works'. Quite often there is an assumption that discipleship can be 'outsourced' to the specialists, the nuns and monks, who will somehow 'make up' for the limited engagement of the rest. Hence, princes endowed monasteries, others made gifts for their support, while a family with a member in 'religion' relied on that person's prayers and penances to act as the discipleship for the group.

While two-tier religion can seem silly when set out in its basic shape, and we might dismiss it as parody of the message of Jesus who did not go off to join the Qumran community but moved about the houses and villages of Galilee, we should note just how deeply embedded this approach is within the Christian religious vision today, if not also within the human religious vision. Anyone thinking seriously about Christian discipleship needs to come to grips with this pervasive religious phenomenon. It seems to make perfect sense that there should be religious specialists. The most basic need of any village is for the specialist in metal working: the smith. Then we can move on to any number of other forms of expertise which are exercised on behalf of the group and we end up with religious specialists who carry out those bits of the Christian vocation beyond the skills of 'ordinary folk'. That every Christian church has specialist ministers is an expression of this, and it can be parodied in the pub-sign of the judge in his wig with the slogan 'I judge all'; the soldier with his gun: 'I defend all'; and the parson in his gown: 'I pray for all'. We shall examine this issue in detail in a later chapter.

From another perspective, this two-tier notion seems to agree with what many see as fundamental to religious consciousness that religion is concerned with 'the wholly other' – and so is to be approached by its disjunction with our experience of the everyday.[1] Indeed, many groups have made such a fetish of this notion of opposition that the more bizarre any practice, dress, or life-choice, the more it is seen as somehow 'spiritual' or 'religious'. But when the 'holy' becomes the 'odd', one wonders if the Creator really does love his creation. Lastly, many of our icons of what is a dedicated Christian life – or even a dedicated religious life – belong to this pattern: they imply that a religious life is clearly different from the 'ordinary'. Can one imagine Pope Francis or Patriarch Bartholomew making reference to their wives (though there was a time when that would have been possible)? Can you imagine the Dalai Lama or Mother Teresa of Calcutta choosing birthday presents as a way to express their love for their grandchildren? Somehow we feel involvement in the nitty gritty of life is somehow alien to 'real' discipleship – but that is a feeling that leads us astray.

The fundamental problem with this two-tier approach – for a Christian – is that it ignores *the* fact of existence: all reality comes from God and depends totally on God for its continuance in being. God is the creator of all: 'in heaven and on earth, seen and unseen' to use the image from an ancient profession of faith. All exists because of his love and without that love there is nothing. Moreover, the divine love is superabundant and so comes to each and everyone. God, as Paul noted quoting a familiar Jewish shorthand, 'shows no partiality' (Rom 2:11). Each has a unique role in the creation and different skills to bring to the community in which that person lives, but the divine society is classless. There is an equal call on every human being to be a disciple, there are no 'other ranks', because God loves each of us, and the whole of our humanity is created and has been embraced by the Christ.

Moreover, the more that any monotheist stresses the 'otherness of the holy' – as distinct from the radical otherness of God – the more that person runs the risk of ignoring the totality of the creation's dependence on God. Down the centuries Christians have often found themselves slipping into a cosmic dualism: 'the divine' versus 'the creation'; 'god' versus 'matter'; order versus chaos; or, simply, light versus darkness. In the face of this temptation, Christians have to embrace the totality of the creation – and love it – because God loves it and has embraced it in Jesus the Anointed One. Matter is already in the order of grace.[2]

[1.] The notion gained fame through the work of Rudolf Otto: *The Idea of the Holy* (Oxford, 1923).

[2.] Loudovikos, *Analogical Identities*, pp. 116–19.

Personal Debit/Credit Accounts

The third very common response to the cost of discipleship is to imagine that we have a personal profit/loss account running with God, possibly with an angel or St Peter, pencil in hand, keeping track of where we stand moment by moment and day by day. It is a perfectly human way to imagine the process: sometimes it is two steps forward and one step back, sometimes the other way around! The aim is to be 'ahead' at the finish, and to have regular audits of the situation, with additional measures to deal with particularly big debts! Not only does it fit with our human way of tackling any large or long-term challenge, it is also very easy to imagine, and very easy to preach. Down the centuries, from religious leaders – Pope Gregory the Great told umpteen catechetical stories based on the notion of gaining credits or making transfer from an account in credit to one in need[3] – to individuals setting up wayside shrines, people have viewed the call 'come, follow me!' in terms of 'what's the state of my balance?'

That this approach falls far short of a true human commitment to discipleship and working for the coming of the Kingdom is fairly obvious. But there are deeper problems with this approach. The credit/debit vision of relationships does not acknowledge the reality of human love and risks making all relationships between people into transactions: if I do this for you, you will give me the *quid pro quo*. Likewise, and historically the great criticism among Christians, this approach makes the relationship with God into a transaction, a piece of trading. God is one more dealer – albeit the biggest and best – in the universe, and so one 'works one's passage' with heaven as the goal and the reward. Rather than rehearse the classical arguments against Pelagianism, it is more useful to recognise that in much of our lives we do relate to one another in a transactional way – as when we go to work or do our shopping. Second, we are creatures of habit and repetition, and we know that in most areas of our lives it is incremental improvements, repeated little steps, that get us to whatever finish line we are aiming at. We all like to know – when an outcome is in the balance – whether things are going well or badly: if a loved one is having an operation in a hospital, there is a real gnawing desire to keep checking on 'how it is going'. Rather than line up ten arguments from the history of western Christianity's theology of grace from Augustine (354–430) to Karl Barth (1886–1968),

---

[3.] His most popular work was *The Dialogues* and many of the stories focus on this way of relating to God.

it is better if we acknowledge that the credit/debit approach fits into the lives and lifestyles of most us very snuggly, and so all of us must be on the watch not to let it get out of hand, whether with those we love or with God.

These three approaches – idealism, two-tier following, and that of a holiness account – are rarely met in anything like their pure forms, rather we find them as blends, and virtually every Christian slips in and out of these mixes as we move through our lives. The challenge is not to vanquish them in argument, which is easily done, but to take account of them within ourselves and seek to follow the way of Jesus in a manner that is closer to the roots of Christian discipleship.

Covenant and Contract

If we imagine our relationship with God in terms of a contract, namely two parties making a deal, where one sets out demands and the other agrees in the light of some benefit (which could be a better world or some *post-mortem* bliss), then discipleship makes no sense. This contractual notion underpins all three of the approaches we have been considering so far in this chapter. But discipleship is better seen as a relationship than as an agreement. Not only are we not loners in the endeavour as we are part of a human community, but we are engaging in this life of discipleship in community with God. We, as it were, join hands with God and with one another, and then set out on the path of following, witnessing, and loving.

God is not another pole in the relationship – as in 'the leader' and 'the led' – but present within our lives. This presence is articulated in many ways. We speak of God's presence within our hearts, the divine light within our minds, and the voice of God in our consciences. Even to speak of God is to be aware of his presence (as *Didache* 4:4 reminds us) and he is so close that we can call on him as 'our Father' even in the silence of our room: 'But when you pray, go into your room and shut the door and pray to your Father who is in secret. And your Father who sees in secret will reward you' (Matt 6:6). Augustine of Hippo would express this closeness by saying: God 'is more intimate to me than I am to myself and higher than my own heights.'[4]

[4.] *Confessiones* 3,6,11.

We also speak in far more explicit ways about Jesus the Christ being present in our midst, saying that Jesus is with us, and walks with us, and even carries us. This belief that when any two disciples are together Jesus – the risen Lord – is present among them is one of the fundamental themes of Christian memory. Moreover, it underpins the whole notion of liturgy, collective prayer, within Christianity. This notion that Christians do not act alone or with reference to a distant God but in a relationship of constant presence is caught in this memory:

> Truly I tell you, whatever you bind on earth will be bound in heaven, and whatever you loose on earth will be loosed in heaven.
>
> Again, truly I tell you that if two of you on earth agree about anything they ask for, it will be done for them by my Father in heaven.
>
> For where two or three gather in my name, there am I with them. (Matt 18:18–20)

This can be paralleled from with Luke's story of the encounter of a group of disciples at Emmaus when they recognise that the risen Jesus is within their company and gathering (Luke 24:13–35). Here, the very notion of resurrection is not focussed on life after death – a very widespread belief within Second Temple Judaism – but that Jesus is still with his followers, and will be with them until the end of time. Indeed, this is the very note that Matthew uses to close his gospel: 'And surely I am with you always, to the very end of the age' (Matt 28:20).

Another way of expressing this divine presence is in terms of the work of the Spirit. The Spirit is worshipped by Christians as hovering over the whole creation – their rereading of Genesis 1 – and being 'the giver of life'. It is a basic element of Christian faith that the Spirit is present in each human heart, bringing enlightenment, and is also the one promised by Jesus who will be the 'advocate', 'counsellor', and giver of strength. Paul presents this presence of the Spirit within the community in terms of him interceding for the disciples in a way that is greater than they could even imagine: 'In the same way, the Spirit helps us in our weakness. We do not know what we ought to pray for, but the Spirit himself intercedes for us through wordless groans' (Rom 8:26). And the Spirit empowers the community with a range of gifts so that their actions are as much the work of the Spirit as of their own abilities:

> Now to each one the manifestation of the Spirit is given for the common good. To one there is given through the Spirit a message of wisdom, to another a message of knowledge by means of the same Spirit, to another faith by the same Spirit, to another gifts of healing by that one Spirit, to another miraculous powers, to another prophecy, to another distinguishing between spirits, to another speaking in different kinds of tongues, and to still another the interpretation of tongues. All these are the work of one and the same Spirit, and he distributes them to each one, just as he determines. (1 Cor 12:7–11)

And because of the Spirit's presence the community has an entire range of fruits that they could not expect if they were simply actors in a contract: 'love, joy, peace, forbearance, kindness, goodness, faithfulness, gentleness and self-control' (Gal 5:22). In virtually every early Christian document we find some reflection on the presence of the Spirit in the company of disciples. While the theological tradition has focussed on collecting all these references with the intention of welding them into a coherent and consistent theology of the Spirit and the Spirit's activity – a pneumatology – it is always worth recalling a statement John the gospel-preacher puts on the lips of Jesus: 'The wind blows wherever it pleases. You hear its sound, but you cannot tell where it comes from or where it is going. So it is with everyone born of the Spirit' (John 3:8). The reality of the Spirit's presence in the fellowship of disciples is what is important – and is always going to be more than we can formalise in words or preaching or theological statements.

For western Christians – all those who like it or not are inheritors of the Latin theological tradition of Augustine – the most common way of expressing this divine presence, assistance, power, and forgiveness within the community of believers is by speaking of 'grace'. 'Grace' has been at the centre of most theological disputes in western Christianity since around 400 – and so even trying to define what we mean by the term has become a major intellectual endeavour. What few of these writers acknowledge is that 'grace' either has to be made just another name for the presence of the Spirit or has to be imagined as some sort of 'insert' involving a range of images from a vaccine to lubrication oil! What is really at stake is that no Christian is alone before God, but in company with all the other disciples we inhabit the divine space and God is lovingly present among us. Only in this context of inspiration, assistance, and forgiveness – this 'amazing grace' – does discipleship become possible. It is this divine presence that can make discipleship both joyful and a relationship of love.

Images of Covenant: Another Testament

How are we to describe and name this situation of self-community-God which is different to every other grouping or arrangement we experience? Indeed, it is not only different but, because it involves the divine, is to an extent beyond words or, at least, precise language. Down the centuries both Jews and Christians have sought image after image to try to grasp it and, on many occasions, have gone too far and missed the mark. The most common range of images is that of a legal agreement – as we saw in Chapter 3 – between people or between nations: the Lord and Israel imaged in a covenant in the same way that two kingdoms would agree an alliance. The story of the covenant with Abram in Genesis 15 is an example of this. Likewise, there have been stories that presented it in terms of a contract between individuals where one person has made an agreement on behalf of the group. The covenant in Exodus 24 has elements of this, as has the promise found in the tale of the renewal of the covenant at Shechem in Joshua 24:1–28. Another legal image is that of the will, the final testament, as in the image of Moses asking the people to choose between the way of life in the Lord's presence and the way of death in his final 'scene' in Deuteronomy 30. All these images were shimmering just below the surface for the first followers of Jesus. Hence we have the images of 'my covenantal blood' in the words of Jesus as presented by Paul (1 Cor 11:25). Similarly, we speak of 'the new testament' – but this usually means no more than a collection of texts, forgetting that new *testament* – as in the legal phrase: 'the last will and testament' – is a reference to this covenant we have with God in Jesus.

Another range of images can be found in the prophets where the relationship, referred to as a 'covenant', is presented in terms of a marriage between God and Israel. In these great myths, the Lord is the ever-faithful spouse while Israel is the unfaithful wife who has had dalliances with the gods of the nations. Hosea is perhaps the best example of this imagery and it can be found again in the Letter to the Ephesians. There, in a household code, the relationship of a wife and husband is located in a context where the covenant between the Christ and the church is to be imagined as a marriage (Eph 5:21–33). Curiously, we read that text as the notion of the divine relationship throwing light on marriage, but the original point was that the marriage relationship can throw light on the range of images we use to try to describe our relationship with God.

Another range of images is that of being participants at a banquet. The Lord makes room at his table and so the invited one is part of the Lord's household and within his care and protection. This is imagery most familiar to Christians from the meal practice and language of Jesus, and hence the final community is imagined in terms of the great banquet: 'I tell you, many will come from east and west and sit at table with Abraham, Isaac and Jacob in the kingdom of heaven' (Matt 8:11).

Taking any one of these images as a description of the situation of discipleship is clearly inadequate, but even when we layer image on image we should not imagine that we have exhausted the topic. The nature of the relationships that make up the covenant community – this divine/human drama, this individual/collective drama – is a mystery: we can only grasp it in parts. It is like standing at one end of a bridge and seeing the direction and first steps towards which the bridge leads, but its full extent is invisible in the distance. This open-endedness of discipleship within the covenant means that the bounds of the relationships can never be circumscribed by a set of organisational markers, whether having the male members of the community circumcised, or having all the members baptised, or imagining that it is confined to those who have subscribed to a particular formula of beliefs. This open-endedness is dreadfully annoying for those who are tidy-minded (and this group seem especially attracted to the organisational echelons of churches), but it is as fundamental to discipleship as that God is creator of all. There can no more be bounds to the divine love than to the divine being, and the Spirit of God is like the wind that blows wherever it pleases.

The Field-Hospital

This raises the issue as to how the disciples can work together to witness to God and to establish the reign of God in our world if there are not clear and tidy boundaries? For some Christians this is resolved by seeing discipleship as markers which set out what is expected to be done and avoided by someone who wants to be a follower of Jesus. It is a tried and trusted method, adopted from Judaism, that has served us well since the beginning, as we see in the *Didache*, and will continue to be part of discipleship. We are creatures of habit and regularities, and having such rules and structures promotes both our following and general harmony.

For other Christians, the key is the formal structures that churches evolve so that they can function: the answer lies in whatever formal role/ status one has, and that has its own set of demands. So the starting point in this case is not a set of 'dos and don'ts' but a list of positions: if a priest, then that sets out what one should do as a disciple; if a monk or nun, then other demands; if a lay-person, then discipleship takes a different shape – it is almost as if what each disciple should do can be looked up in a book. Again, the churches need formal structures of ministry, and the demands of these structures will be part of any individual's response to the divine invitation, but that response can never be equated with such structures. The individuality of discipleship – each is 'called by name' (Isa 43:1) – and its open-endedness entail that discipleship cannot be programmed.

Can we approach the subject in terms of an image? One image that has attracted Christians historically is that of the haphazard nature of how we are called to patch up the wounded, the sick, the unfortunate, and even the downright stupid because part of forgiveness is that we pass over their silliness. The origins of this way of viewing discipleship are to be found in a story given by Luke (10:25–37) which sought to explore the porous boundaries of the need to love one's neighbour as oneself as demanded by Leviticus 19:18. One's 'neighbour' is anything but a predicable category and one often only discovers that person accidentally as one walks along a road. The demands of that chance encounter determine the call of discipleship there and then. It comes to no one other than you – because you are the person on the spot – and it comes 'out the blue' – it seems no more than an accident. Yet, the belief in a divine providence, and that God is present within our relationships, means that one's actions are part of the whole pattern of the creation.

The field-hospital bandaging and helping the wounded amidst the messiness, craziness, and downright wickedness of life, as exemplified in our human obsession with warfare and military display, is an image in this tradition of the story of the Samaritan who helped the wounded traveller on the roadside. It is an image much favoured by Pope Francis and those who talk about 'Messy Church' and it has the benefit that it is not dependent, as so many discipleship images are, on a neat and orderly view of the Christian life. We do what we can, we relieve suffering, we make things that little bit better for those who are suffering, and we keep at it. While there is plenty of room for the planned systems that will mitigate and perhaps remove the sources of suffering and injustice, there is also what we can do right now. In this scenario, the church is not the gathering of the elect, the chosen ones, but the collective name of all who are seeking to make a difference for the better as we move along the road of our lives, which we might also designate 'the Way of Life' or our 'pilgrim path'.

The challenge is not that of hearing 'the voice of God' and obeying it, as found within a great religious system, but 'listening out' for the needs of those around us and seeking to act in a helpful way that is characterised by a forgiving and healing generosity. For the disciples, there is the added awareness that, as they are acting with those they see around them, so God is acting among us all. Living and acting in this ill-defined and messy universe, day after day, is often the greatest challenge of discipleship. It is far more attractive for many people to think of their discipleship as being part of a well-oiled organisation with clear doctrines, goals, and operating procedures that confront the fractured nature of our everyday lives. But discipleship is perhaps better likened to being willing to volunteer in a field-hospital.

Figure 10. A study in equality.

Here a community has sought to adapt an historical space so that the table is central to the assembly. This is a church which imagines itself as sisters and brothers engaged in a common table prayer.

Trying to come to grips with this – that we carry out our discipleship through being servants of one another in need – has been a theme within Christian thinking since this advice by an early teacher named John:

> We love, because he first loved us. If anyone says, 'I love God,' and hates his brother, he is a liar; for he who does not love his brother whom he has seen, cannot love God whom he has not seen. And this commandment we have from him, that he who loves God should love his brother also. (1 John 4:19–21)

Chapter 6

Bonding as Disciples

Gathered around the Common Table

One of the key scenes within the memory of Christians is the supper of Jesus with the disciples that took place just before his arrest and death. It is a memory that is not only seared visually into Christian memory – Leonardo's image has become the source of a thousand imitations – but is invoked every day in Christian worship with words like 'on the night before he suffered' and this is presented as part of a deliberate recollection of that supper to fulfil a command of Jesus: 'do this in memory of me' (1 Cor 11:24). Not only is it remembered by the disciples, but it has to be recalled by them.

That supper, commonly referred to 'the Last Supper', has to be set in several levels of context. First, it is part of the deliberate memory of the community because that evening is a major element in all four canonical gospels. The final meal was seen as the culmination of the time that the disciples had spent following Jesus from – in the different journey narratives of those texts – the time in Galilee to that moment in Jerusalem. They saw this particular meal as a prestige encounter with Jesus as the one who established a covenant for his followers with the Father. This theme is one of the earliest expressions we have of Jesus establishing a covenant between God and his disciples, for it was apparently already an established theme when Paul wrote to the Corinthians.

Second, that final meal has its own larger context in the whole sequence of meals that Jesus had where he sat at table, not only teaching but establishing a community of disciples.[1] The community who listened to those gospels was expected to discover its own identity as disciples at table in the accounts of Jesus at table in the houses of Pharisees, sinners, in great open-air meals that gave welcome and hospitality to any who came, and these took place both before his death and after his resurrection. To be a disciple meant knowing that meals were important in disciples' memory, and that the Last Supper was but the high point in the memory of the meals of Jesus.

Third, it must be set in the context of the practices of the communities of disciples who told those stories to themselves to explain their identity. The early communities did not just talk about the meals the first disciples had with Jesus, they themselves gathered for real meals and saw this as a regular, indeed weekly, aspect of the following. We know this from a variety of sources from over a series of generations of disciples. Our earliest direct evidence is Paul complaining about abuses in the meal in Corinth (and probably elsewhere) and this comes from the period before the destruction of the Temple in Jerusalem. Then we have guidance on the meal and its prayers that come from the *Didache*. This document reflects very early practice – certainly from before the destruction of the Temple – but like all 'practical texts' it may have elements from a longer time-span and so reflect a wider range of practices. In the community of The Way, this meal was both a celebration of identity and a collective act of worship. From the early second century we have the witness of Pliny the Younger that gathering for this meal was a characteristic activity by which this illegal sect manifested its collective nature. Then, in the middle of the second century, we have the idealised description of such a disciples' meal from Justin the Martyr. Because we are so familiar with merely token eating and drinking at our very explicitly 'religious' events, we find it hard to even imagine that the activity of eating together in the name of the Lord could be an act of worship. While some theologians have seen the meal as simply 'the context' in which religiously significant elements first appeared and which was then 'highlighted' by the meal's disappearance, the reverse is the case: the highly condensed 'religious' ritual is all that was left when the socially demanding meal with fellow disciples was skipped, and then abandoned. It was fine to claim all the other baptised were 'sisters' and 'brothers', but actually sharing food,

---

[1.] D.E. Smith, *From Symposium to Eucharist: The Banquet in the Early Christian World* (Minneapolis, MN, 2003).

intimately and side by side, with slaves, with Jews/Gentiles (or vice versa), one's clients, the poor (who seemingly were taking advantage of getting a free meal – how shocking!), and with impure women was just going too far.

Fourth, this practice has to be set within the practice of meals as worship within Judaism. Eating together had long been a way in which religiously significant events were celebrated, whether these were great one-off events such as the dedication of the Temple, or annual festivals such as Pentecost, or the weekly meal which began the Sabbath. The Lord loved and provided for his people, and so eating together enacted that love and, following the injunction of Deuteronomy 8:7–10, the Creator was blessed before the meal for the gift of the food. God was blessed again at the meal's end; and this second 'grace' was for the gift of the enjoyment of the food and the pleasure of the meal. Jesus grew up in a culture that saw meals – all of them – as religious moments, a culture which had a deep and rich mythology of the lavish banquets that the Lord provided for the people of the covenant by which they were made his houseguests, and he saw meals as central to his own message of discipleship.

Figure 11. It is about a loaf of bread.
The distinctive action of Jesus was that he wanted his disciples
to share a loaf – this was the detail of his thanking God that they
recalled. Not only has the basic action been buried under later conflicts
of interpretation, but for many Christians even the basic shape of a loaf is
forgotten through the use of individualistic, small round wafers.

Fifth, any talk about the meal of Christian discipleship has to be set in the context of meals – deliberately preparing and sharing food together – as a fundamental aspect of our humanity. Most of the energy of most humans for most of the time of human history has been devoted to the gathering, storing, transporting, preparation, and consumption of meals. If discipleship is to be located in the real lives of humans, then there must be a meal dimension to it. If matter is part of the order of grace, then no part of matter can be so representative of that grace as the food which sustains us in life, and by sharing which we are sustained as a community.

The Grim, Dark Paradox of Discipleship

A basic element of any meal whose participants come from a wider network than a nuclear family is that the meal not only witnesses to common bonds, but creates these bonds, restores them, and strengthens them. Even in cultures where social interaction is minimal and whose religious ideology makes little claim to the value of collective unity – or even sees such as a religious weakness – we find that there are collective meals and, in spite of religious theory, these meals bond the communities and help them to understand themselves and their problems.[2] Meals create community, draw us together, give us joy in common, and give us a vision of a greater joy – even if we glimpse it but for a moment.

It is not surprising, therefore, that from the time of the *Didache* and Paul, the notion of meals which unite us as disciples has been a central element in our reflection. We are scattered people gathered into one and transformed, we are one body because we have eaten of one loaf, and we repeatedly proclaim that we are gathered into unity with the Christ by the Holy Spirit. Yet the simple fact is that there is no more divisive moment for Christians than when they gather for the meal, there is no topic on which they will more readily condemn and attack one another, and the two largest nameable bodies of Christians – eastern Orthodoxy and western Catholicism – are, *de facto*, far more likely to reject sharing the meal with any Christian who is 'not one of them' than to see it as the

---

[2.] See S.B. Ortner, *Sherpas through their Rituals* (Cambridge, 1978), pp. 61–90, who examined how the Sherpas found their meals key bonding events despite the fact that such collective feasting was a distraction from the personal quest to escape from matter.

banquet of the Lord's welcome. The meal of gathering has become the moment of othering. The means of unifying disciples actually acts as the source of division.

Not surprisingly, many who want to be disciples but spared the history of division, the bitterness, and the endless, often sterile, debates become suspicious of any mention of 'eucharist', 'holy communion', 'mass', or 'Lord's Supper'. Why not just be friends, be willing to share a cup of coffee, and skip the most divisive hour in the Christian week? Moreover, many communities of Christians, mainly those coming from the evangelical wing of the Reformation, seem to get along quite well without all these worries and if occasionally they do have a re-enactment to the fulfil the command 'do this' they see it as teaching-by-doing rather than an event in its own right. The common meal as eucharist seems to present more problems than it is worth – this was brought home to me some years ago when relaxing with an American friend whose expertise was preparing discipleship programmes for his church. He joked: 'let's spend time on something futile and divisive: let's talk about the eucharist'.

We are left with two problems. First, if we want our discipleship to have some visible continuity and similarity to early discipleship, then we have to come to grips with the fact that they, back then, never saw themselves as being more committed to the community than at the community meal. As Luke, writing in the early second century, tried to summarise: 'And they devoted themselves to the apostles' teaching and to fellowship, to the breaking of the loaf, and to prayer' (Acts 2:42). But can we even think about the common meal of thanking the Father in union with Jesus without a replay of over a millennium's worth of fighting?

Second, can we take up the challenge of being disciples without being ready to do what is basic to the eucharist: being willing to share a meal that bridges divisions while thanking the Father for his goodness to us in drawing us to him through Jesus? Disciples today have to address this question yet, alas, many – across the churches – do not see there is a problem. What follows is my attempt to take up the challenge, but I write it conscious that when I sketched it out before groups of ministers who see presiding at such meals, or token meals, as central to their work, many considered the whole endeavour worthless. They believe that one has simply to continue with current practice (which is imagined as divinely given) and repeat current explanations (usually mid-twentieth century reworkings of sixteenth-century debates). However, even if one takes that position, then, at least, one should acknowledge another phenomenon: the language and actions of today are so dissonant with pristine memory that is claimed in the early churches that many Christians sense a yawning chasm, a disruption, between the language of their liturgies and their experience. Remembering can often reveal just how much we have forgotten.

Food Sharing is Powerful

Once, many years ago, as I was going into a college refectory for lunch – it was in the United Theological College in Bengaluru in India – a small brown wooden sign caught my attention. It had simply these four words:

FOOD SHARED
POWER RELEASED

What a splendid summary of a truth known to all wise human beings: we learn to be human and grow as humans whenever we share food.

My question now is this: could this is the starting point in a renewal of our celebrations as Christians when we gather eucharistically? It is often said that 'we are what we eat' – but while it is true that without food we would die, it is also true that we are much more than what we eat. Likewise, it is clear that, without human cooperation and the sharing of resources, we could not survive; and the most basic of human working together is that which obtains foodstuffs and then prepares them for our consumption. But it is equally important to note that, except in a few exceptional cases and in emergencies, we never eat our food completely raw: humans always process foodstuffs into food by preparation and then cooking. Moreover, when food is in a fit state for eating, it is then presented – this might be as simple as placing it on some form of plate – before we eat it. This fact of preparation, cooking, and presenting means that food cannot be separated from human culture. We should also note that food preparation generally involves a group and food is cooked and presented for a group of people, and so food is inseparable from society. Because of these links between society, culture, and food, we need to recognise that our food means much more to us than simply our survival. Food for humans is about our identity, it expresses our hopes, desires, and fears, and it is significant in every human exchange.

Food is even more significant for our identity as humans: we are the only animals who process and cook our food and, therefore, need to collaborate closely in these processes. So it constitutes us both as humans and members of society. While other animals may hunt together and/or eat together, we human are the only animals who *share* meals. It is not simply 'my food' and 'your food' eaten in proximity at the same time, it is *our* meal and we are participants in the human event which is far more than the total of individuals.

Meals shared mean far more to us than simply the convenience of gathering, processing, and cooking as a team. Meals are the markers of every valuable human moment: we share meals to mark our relationships, the key moments in our lives, and we bond to one another in the sharing. Uniquely, we are *meal-sharing animals.*

That we humans, and only us humans, are the meal-sharing animals is so taken for granted that we can overlook it as a fact within the creation. But if we are to attune ourselves to the *missio Dei* – that God is always and everywhere seeking to communicate his love and his vision for the creation to us humans – then taking this aspect of our creaturehood seriously is an important first step. So if we are engaged in mission – that is, bringing the light of the gospel into the dark areas of life rather than seeking recruits for our particular religion – one of the challenges is to see how God is present there before us, speaking before we speak, and acting before we act. It is the argument of this book that every group of meal-sharers, and every real human group is meal sharing, is not just engaged in an everyday ('secular') or practical activity, but is relating within the creation is such a way that the presence of God is at work there. The task of the Christian preacher is to help them to discover this existing presence, and then, if they are moved to respond to this presence, to help them to imagine what they are doing, what it means, and to observe how their meal sharing may be one step on their path towards God. Put another way, mission presupposes a common human language, 'language' here being a metaphor for a whole range of common concerns and interests, within which there can be a meeting between human beings; and concerns about food and meals are one of those basic human languages.

Before we can look at what meal sharing says about the relationship of humanity with God, we need to remind ourselves about what our own sharing of meals, and of the food which provides the material for those meals, means within our Christian memory.

Our Deep Memories of Food

Food and Trust

Food is used in the scriptures to express Israel's trust in God: 'The eyes of all look to you, and you give them their food in due season' (Ps 145:15); while the basic care of God is expressed in the vision that God has provided humanity with food (Gen 1:29–30). In the other creation story they have to labour and till the ground to eat bread (Gen 3:19), but in preparing food humanity is falling in with the divine plan.

Food is precious and also precarious: famine can destroy humanity – and it can symbolise all that is destructive in human society (Rev 6:8). So the people must ask God for their food: 'Behold, the eye of the Lord is on those who fear him, on those who hope in his steadfast love, that he may deliver their soul from death, and keep them alive in famine' (Ps 33:18–19). Food is, in turn, the sign of the Father's care for each of us:

> What father among you, if his son asks for a fish, will instead of a fish give him a serpent; or if he asks for an egg, will give him a scorpion? If you then, who are evil, know how to give good gifts to your children, how much more will the heavenly Father give the Holy Spirit to those who ask him! (Luke 11:11–13)

And so we pray each day: 'give us this day our daily bread'.

Food and Justice

One cannot be moral and ignore the shared reality of food. The true act of worship, your 'fast', is 'to share your bread with the hungry' (Isa 58:7), and 'if you pour yourself out for the hungry and satisfy the desire of the afflicted, then shall your light rise in the darkness and your gloom be as the noonday' (Isa 58:10). The righteous one 'gives his bread to the hungry' (Ezek 18:7 and 16) and the disciple sees the Lord in the hungry and thirsty and knows that in serving the hungry and the thirsty they are serving the Lord (Matt 25:34–45).

Since food is a matter of existence any injustice relating to it – such that others do not have enough good food – is a matter of sin, social and personal. The Christian is called explicitly to see that everyone has a share in the earth's riches for otherwise some are gathering to themselves what God intends for all. In a world where there are hundreds of millions who rise each morning hungry and where food can be 'weaponised' in 'resource wars', we Christians do not need to read the story of the Rich

Man and Lazarus (Luke 16:18–23) as a complex spiritual message: it shouts out to us to link faith, food, and justice as a central part of our message.

Food and Inclusion

One of the simplest ways to form a boundary separating those within a group from those outside it is through the use of food. If you eat *that* food, you are not one of us. If you are one of us, then you must eat only *this* food. Yet we have the memory of Acts 10:9–16 when a heavenly voice declared: 'What God has cleansed, you must not call common.' Likewise, one can separate by having pure and impure food (and pure and impure ways of presenting food for eating) marking group boundaries. Again we have a memory of Jesus pointing out that it is not what enters a human being, but what comes out of a person, that creates impurity – thus 'all food is clean' (Mark 7:1–23).

Nothing can declare a chasm between fellow humans like an exclusion from a table. If you are part of the 'in group', then you are one of those who has a seat at the table and can eat with the rest of the group. Contrariwise, if you are in any doubts that you are an outsider, they will be quickly confirmed by the unwillingness of the group to have you at their table. It is not an accident that groups that desire a high degree of group loyalty, *esprit de corps*, and 'group think' are those who have complex rules about who can, and cannot, eat with them. At the time of Jesus we find complex rules about who Pharisees could eat with lest they compromise their desire to have priestly purity, we find complex rules about who can and cannot eat in Qumran,[3] and we even have the reminder in John's gospel that eating/drinking was a way of separating Jews and Samaritans (John 4:9). In stark contrast we have the example of Jesus – and a willingness to eat with outsiders that was scandalous. He will sit at table with Pharisees (Luke 11:37), then with tax collectors (Luke 19:1–10), then with sinners (Luke 15:2): there seem to have been no boundaries Jesus was unwilling to break. The kingdom – and therefore its great banquet – was to open to all: 'Truly I tell you, the tax collectors and the prostitutes are going into the kingdom of God' (Matt 21:31).

This open commensality was a challenge to his first followers and the results were mixed. On the one hand we find in Acts an emphasis on the meal of mission that welcomes outsiders to the table,[4] on the other, we

---

[3.]   L.H. Schiffman, *The Eschatological Community of the Dead Sea Scrolls: A Study of the Rule of the Congregation* (Atlanta, GA, 1989), pp. 50–67.

[4.]   See O'Loughlin, 'Sharing Food and Breaking Boundaries'.

have disciples worrying about food and boundaries, and fretting that they only want to eat with their own. Food, and our Christian manners at meals, is a constant challenge to us still today. It is far easier to repeat the early Christian slogan that God wills all to be saved (1 Tim 2:4) than to say that we are willing to share our table with the poor, the despised, and the other.

Food and Thankfulness

Our dependence on food not only parallels our dependence on God for our existence and the existence of the whole creation, but it is the most frequent moment when we can recognise that dependence. Knowing that we are in such a relationship of dependence becomes the starting point for all prayer: we worship God in thanking him for all his gifts – and this totality is focused in our thanksgiving for our food. The Lord brings us into being, sustains us in being, and brings our being to perfection – and we engage with this mystery when we bless God for what we have before us at our meals. This is captured in a single line in Deuteronomy: 'You shall eat your fill and bless the Lord your God for the good land that he has given you' (8:10). When we eat we bless God for his goodness to us: the actual food is both a proof of this, and it represents all that he has given us.

We find Jesus blessing the Father at table and then inviting those with him to share in a loaf and drink from a common cup – and this practice became the central event around which his followers gathered and celebrated his memory. The shared meal, the meal of thanksgiving, is the core event of Christian ritual. When Christians have made the eucharist into a ritual game and a source of theological argument, they have invariably lost sight of this basic fact: it is when Christians share a meal that the Lord is among them. The Anointed One is at their elbow as they sit around a common table, praise and bless the Father for all his gifts in creation and in sending us the Christ, and then share the common loaf and drink from the common cup. Shared meals are of no small importance among the disciples of Jesus.

Meals and the Work of Jesus

Is this linking of food, meals, and Christianity something that we can say is intrinsic to Christian faith; or is it just an accident of the fact that human beings need to eat food and the simplest way to do that is to eat in common? A glance at the gospels presents us with meal sharing as a central aspect of the life of Jesus offered to us by the evangelists as an intrinsic part of our discipleship.

One of the typical settings in which Jesus is presented, in all four of the canonical gospels, is at a meal. The highpoint of his presence among his followers is portrayed in context of the Passover meal we call 'the Last Supper'. Let us begin with John's gospel. There the narrative begins with a marriage meal in Cana and ends it with an equally wondrous meal after the resurrection, at daybreak on the shore of the Sea of Galilee, preceded by Jesus' invitation: 'come and have breakfast' (John 21:12).[5] Meal scenes account for around a quarter of this gospel.[6] When we turn to the Synoptics we find the same interest. Apart from the final Passover meal, there are meals in houses, meals in the open air, stories focussed on meals such as that of the Parable of the Prodigal Son (Luke 15:2–32 – and note that the meal-scene of the parable is a response to an objection to the commensality of Jesus) and information about meals (e.g. Luke 14:9). Besides the report of Jesus' manner of blessing the Father and then sharing a loaf and cup with those with him at table (Mark 14:22 and parallels), there were scandal-giving occasions when Jesus ate with sinners and tax collectors which are announcements of the in-breaking kingdom (e.g. Matt 9:10–13), and the post-resurrection meal at Emmaus (Luke 24:13–35). In all four gospels, Jesus is portrayed as present at meals and engaged in this ministry by teaching at meals. This ubiquity of meals compels us to recognise a basic fact about the Christian proclamation: it was originally heard at community meals. It was when the community gathered for a meal that they blessed the Father, 'through the Christ',[7] and there they heard those travelling performers whose narrating of the significance of Jesus, what they referred to as 'the gospel', earned for them the title of 'the gospellers'. Shared meals are not only at the centre of human culture, but at the centre of Christian identity. Indeed, if the

---

5. The question as to whether John 21 is an addition to the gospel is irrelevant here because we have no evidence that the gospel ever circulated without this chapter; and, equally, if this was not part of the original performances by a travelling evangelist named John, the material must come from a similar early situation and so furnish additional evidence for the importance of meals within the earliest churches.

6. E. Kobel, *Dining with John: Communal Meals and Identity Formation in the Fourth Gospel and its Historical and Cultural Context* (Leiden, 2011).

7. See *Didache* 9:2 and 9:4.

early churches had not gathered at meals at which letters were read aloud and performances of the memory of Jesus given by the evangelists, we might not have the collection we refer to as 'the New Testament'. The actual new testament/covenant was performed in a community meal.[8]

Shared Meals and Mission

If you have followed my argument thus far, I hope you will agree that meal sharing is something that is central to Christian discipleship not simply in an accidental way but in a positive and explicit manner. You cannot be a Christian and not be concerned with food, justice about food, sharing it, blessing God for it, and taking part with others in meals in which the Father is praised through Jesus the Christ. But food (collaborating in obtaining it) and sharing meals (rejoicing with food and making it a central element in human ritual) is a basic link with all humanity. As such, food and meal sharing can be a common ground in mission. Meal sharing normally sets up borders, but for Christians it can be the basis of dialogue.

If we have a *Christian vision* of all humanity as being called by God to the great eschatological banquet, we need a corresponding *human vision* of all humanity sharing the planet's resources justly and sharing a common meal. Just as the great banquet is an image of the salvation that is God's gift, so the human meal is the vision of economic justice, ecological responsibility, and peace making that we need to work for. But we might start with some questions.

First, we need to ask questions of ourselves as Christians. Before we can use meal sharing as a common human 'language' to dialogue over matters of ultimate concern, we need to check our own use of this language to make sure that we are not just clanging cymbals and noisy gongs. As we begin to recognise the crisis of our planet we have to ask ourselves if we think of the creation as a network within which we collaborate – and this actually touches us when it comes to food production – or do we look on it as a source of plunder? Similarly, we

---

8. This has been explored by many scholars in recent years; good starting points are D.E. Smith and H.E. Taussig, *Many Tables: The Eucharist in the New Testament and Liturgy Today* (London, 1990); and B. Chilton, *Many Tables: The Eucharist in the New Testament and Liturgy Today* (London, 1994).

Figure 12. Being thankful to the Father with Jesus is part of everyday life for disciples.

This painting, *Das Abendmahl unter Tage* [The Eucharist Underground], is a piece of public art on an underpass in Westerholt, Germany. Painted in 2011 by Helmut Dellmann, it commemorates the local miners. It presents the eucharist not only as an activity of the People of God in union with Jesus, but as an incarnational event. Rather than occurring in a sacred space apart, it enters into the workspace and transforms that location into a place of divine encounter and an experience of community rejoicing.

need to think of the creation as a gift – never more obvious than when we sit down together at a meal – for which we bless God, or do we think of ourselves as masters and makers of our reality?

We make claims that God shows no partiality and loves all equally; we call other humans our sisters and brothers; and we shout about a wonderful future that is the Father's gift. If this is more than words, then we have to be active campaigners for food justice – otherwise, our partiality in action betrays our proclamation as worthless.

Then we come to the witness we give in worship. Do we welcome all to the Lord's table? Sadly, many Christians use the eucharist as a means of setting theological boundaries: can we do this and proclaim the welcome of the Christ in a creditable way? Do we have to the courage to challenge those fellow Christians who use the Lord's meal in this way to ask themselves basic questions about discipleship? But what of our own community? Are there those whom we would not welcome because we have an exclusive rather than an inclusive vision of Christian faith? Earlier in this chapter I recalled a moment in India. One other moment has stayed with me: in a Catholic church there I found two lines for communion: one for 'ordinary' Christians and one for Dalit Christians. Discipleship as sharing is difficult.[9]

Second, we need to ask questions about the meals and meal rituals of those around us. What way do those around us celebrate with food? Do they offer a prayer of thanksgiving for their food as a gift? If so, this is a basic link in faith we have in common. Do they have a sense that the enjoyment of a shared meal is either a little taste of the goodness of the universe or a basis for expressing wonder and dependence on the divine? If so, this is, at a deep level, an awareness of God's mission in the universe and in the human heart.

Not only do most religions promote domestic rituals surrounding food and sharing meals,[10] very often with a formal religious dimension,[11] but many take meal sharing a step further: meals become an explicit part of the group's ritual life. What does that gathering and eating together mean for them? What longings and vision of the universe does it express? A great communal meal expresses a vision of human solidarity which might be open – and so a builder of bridges – or it might be closed – and be a builder of barriers. In the very act of asking these questions and sharing with others our own Christian vision of meal sharing we are proclaiming the gospel.

Where do we Start?

Humans are never indifferent to food. Military experts concerned with 'food security' demonstrate this with a cynical dictum: 'civilisation is only three meals from chaos'. Anyone with religious awareness sees this link between food and belief systems in the way that in most religions there are foods that are prescribed and forbidden, there are times to eat and to fast, and there are special times with feasts. The foods that we share in our meals are not only vehicles of fats, carbohydrates, and proteins, but bearers of memory, identity, and inclusion/exclusion.

---

9. See A.S. Raj, 'Dalits at the Eucharistic Table', *Japan Mission Journal*, 68/1 (2014), pp. 9–14.

10. M. Visser, *The Rituals of Dinner: The Origins, Evolution, Eccentricities, and Meaning of Table Manners* (London, 1993).

11. M. Jones, *Feast: Why Humans Share Food* (Oxford, 2007).

Moreover, food and meal sharing are the everyday reality. Within hours of reading this chapter, you will be involved in eating, drinking, and probably a participant in a shared meal. How will we react to that meal? That meal could be a special moment in your discipleship.

If I were a humanist I might respond by saying 'we are what we eat' and think of it as simply fuel. But as a theist it is more than fuel: it is receiving the gift of God – a participation in a basic act of divine grace. As a disciple of Jesus it is a moment to join with him in a sacrifice of praise, thanking the Father for his love, and a recollection of the meals of Jesus, the meals of the church, and the final banquet. As someone called to live the gospel, it is a reminder of my duties in justice to share equally the gifts with every other human being whom I can call a sister and a brother, and whom I am willing to welcome to my table.

Perhaps we might then adopt as our prayer that found in one of our earliest Christian texts:

After you all have had enough to eat, give thanks in this way:

> We give you thanks, holy Father, for your holy name which you have made to dwell in our hearts, and for the knowledge and faith and immortality which you have made known to us.
> Through Jesus, your servant, to you be glory forever.
> You are the mighty ruler of all who has created all for your name's sake, and you have given food and drink to human beings for their enjoyment so that they might give thanks to you. But to us, from your generosity, you have given spiritual food and drink, and life eternal, through your servant.
> Above all things we give thanks to you because you are mighty: to you be glory forever.
> Remember, Lord, your church, deliver her from evil, make her complete in your love, and gather her from the four winds into your kingdom you have prepared for her, for yours is the power and the glory forever.
> May grace come and may this world pass away.
> Hosanna to the God of David.
> If anyone is holy, let him advance; if anyone is not, let him be converted.
> Maranatha. Amen.[12]

---

12. *Didache*, 10; and see O'Loughlin, *The Didache,* pp. 85–104.

So, I want to return now to that brilliant wall plaque already mentioned. 'Food shared, power released' is a lapidary shorthand for a basic truth about humanity and faith. We might expand this: whenever human beings gather for a meal, this is an occasion when the power of the Spirit is active among them.

We will enrich our discipleship when we join hands around the Lord's table.

Chapter 7

Called to Service

Discipleship and Ministry

Compared with the focussed individualism of the mystery religions, with their attention to individual enlightenment into the secret mysteries and personal salvation within a spiritual realm, Christianity must have appeared a poor rival for the affections of a religiously minded Gentile in the Graeco-Roman world. There is a startling absence of a wondrous superlunary universe or a cosmology that might explain destinies – there is a hint of astrology in the story of the Magi but it is only an incidental strand of the overall narrative of the birth of Jesus (Matt 2:1–12); hardly a word about spheres, stars, or omens; and no sure-fire recipes for a long, healthy, wealthy, and happy life. Put another way, there is not a single document from the early followers of Jesus that would merit space in the 'consciousness/self-help' shelf of an airport's bookshop today. Nor were there any experiential 'highs' to be had in the initiation rites – some sort of public bath might be a curiosity for onlookers, but would not have been seen as exciting in the way that initiations into the Mithraic cult were.[1] The group's gathering was but a meal – and a socially awkward one – and one would not liken it to a performance of achieved social status, much less an orgy. Likewise, in comparison with Jewish apocalyptic preaching, Christianity did not promise a great glorious restoration of a mythic past, nor vengeance and retribution for

---

[1.] M. Meyer, *The Mithras Liturgy* (Princeton, NJ, 2006).

the godless. Some people of an apocalyptic outlook, possibly those who were descended from disciples of John the Baptist, did become followers of Jesus and they have left their mark in the apocalyptic passages in the gospels and other early writings,[2] but this was a minor rather than a dominant strain of thought. By the period after the destruction of the Temple, the Christian movement had to come to terms with the fact that the end of time and/or return of the Christ was not an imminent prospect. Likewise, some sort of restoration of a glorious Israel was not on the immediate time-horizon: so much that was important to everyone who believed in the God of Israel (be they followers of Jesus or not) lay in ruins that any claim about a great manifestation of God's power in the material world would have seemed ludicrous.[3] It was becoming ever clearer that Christian discipleship was going to mean commitment for the long haul and generous commitment to a way of life, indeed to the Way of Life, with few if any visible, this-worldly, benefits. Now, not only would it be a way of life, but a way of the cross: 'Whoever wants to be my disciple must deny themselves and take up their cross and follow me' (Matt 16:24).

What would it look like? Well, once again, Matthew 25:31–46 is the best summary of what this way and its final destination would look like.

> But when the Son of Man comes in his glory, and all the angels with him, then he will sit upon his glorious throne. All the nations will be gathered in his presence, and he will separate the people as a shepherd separates the sheep from the goats. He will place the sheep at his right hand and the goats at his left.
>
> Then the King will say to those on his right, 'Come, you who are blessed by my Father, inherit the Kingdom prepared for you from the creation of the world. For I was hungry, and you fed me. I was thirsty, and you gave me a drink. I was a stranger, and you invited me into your home. I was naked, and you gave me clothing. I was sick, and you cared for me. I was in prison, and you visited me.'

---

[2] A. Yarbro Collins, 'Apocalypses and Apocalypticism: Early Christian', in D.N. Freedman (ed.), *The Anchor Bible Dictionary* (New York, 1992), vol. 1, pp. 288–92.

[3] P. Avis, 'The Paschal Mystery and the Church', *Ecclesiology*, 17 (2021), pp. 3–6.

Then these righteous ones will reply, 'Lord, when did we ever see you hungry and feed you? Or thirsty and give you something to drink? Or a stranger and show you hospitality? Or naked and give you clothing? When did we ever see you sick or in prison and visit you?'

And the King will say, 'I tell you the truth, when you did it to one of the least of these my brothers and sisters, you were doing it to me!'

Then the King will turn to those on the left and say, 'Away with you, you cursed ones, into the eternal fire prepared for the devil and his demons. For I was hungry, and you didn't feed me. I was thirsty, and you didn't give me a drink. I was a stranger, and you didn't invite me into your home. I was naked, and you didn't give me clothing. I was sick and in prison, and you didn't visit me.'

Then they will reply, 'Lord, when did we ever see you hungry or thirsty or a stranger or naked or sick or in prison, and not help you?' And he will answer, 'I tell you the truth, when you refused to help the least of these my brothers and sisters, you were refusing to help me.'

And they will go away into eternal punishment, but the righteous will go into eternal life.

The Son of Man will come, there will be a great regathering when the people scattered over the earth – a prophetic image that is central to the *Didache*'s eucharistic vision[4] – will take place, but that is all 'in the future'. It is not an event on anyone's calendar. The challenge of discipleship is, by contrast, close in time, a present reality, and has to take effect today and tomorrow. Discipleship is very much a matter that can be located within one's calendar. This is service to one another: feeding, clothing, healing, and helping. Moreover, it is not just to the known few or the circle of other disciples; it reaches out like the divine love to all humanity. The universe will be renewed, but today the disciples must renew this world. Each day the disciples are faced by the choice between the Two Ways: this way of service to humanity is the way to eternal life, the rejection of service to others is the way to eternal punishment. Matthew has taken the Deuteronomy choice of

---

4. It presents the broken loaf as being the regathered people.

covenant theme which is at the centre of so much teaching – whether in Qumran or the *Didache* – and placed it in a neat, sharply focused story put into the voice of the Master himself.

Serving One Another

However, service can be a deceptive word! Since there is invariably inequality in societies, and there are always power dynamics at play – even in families – 'service' can become a cover for what a master gives to the servant or a 'big person' gives to the client. We can fool ourselves that structures of domination are actually charitable acts. Aristocracy, slavery, colonialism, and spiritual bullying can all be presented, and indeed have been, under the guise of 'Christian service'. Rather than being seen as a way of life that promotes a whole new vision of how

Figure 13. The Jesus paradigm is counter-cultural.
This is an illustration for Jn 13 from a manuscript from Ethiopia. It concentrates on remembering the action of Jesus, but fails to remind the viewer of the punchline: his washing their feet was to show them that they had to wash each other's feet. Even in our deliberate remembering, we are selective and forgetful.

people could live with and relate to one another, Christianity has been condemned as one more religion that merely put a glove on the fist of power. This critique was famously made by Karl Marx:

> The social principles of Christianity justified the slavery of Antiquity, glorified the serfdom of the Middle Ages and equally know, when necessary, how to defend the oppression of the proletariat, although they make pitiful face over it.[5]

We can all find examples of the tendency of the churches to represent the 'respectable' core of society which does not want the social or economic boat rocked in any significant way. Looking at the outward displays of religion is often to observe pyramid structures of command and control: it may think of itself as service, but it is the service of governing others. Even pious Catholics, for example, raise their eyebrows when they hear some of the official titles of the pope because they are aware that a statement like 'now gloriously reigning' jars with the designation: 'servant of the servants of God'. And similar contradictions between the vision of service and the reality of power can be found in most churches. But these inconsistencies between preaching and practice become even more pointedly absurd when we look at the statements on the relative status of members within the community as such groups are imagined within the preaching of the evangelists.

All four of the canonical gospels assume that part of the insight of Jesus which is to be taken up by his followers is a complete inversion of social values and a rejection of social stratification. These communities were, explicitly, to be unlike their surrounding society in precisely one way: they were not to engage in a power pyramid nor a status ladder. Each assembly was to model a different way of relating. This was not only a good thing in itself, but was to be seen as consonant with the saving work of the Christ, and even with the divine plan for the creation. Modelling the new set of relationships was to be part of their message to the surrounding world.

The inversion is not simply a lifestyle matter, nor a piece of moral advice for a better world, but at the core of how the new community must exist and understand itself. The theme is first seen in Mark (9:33–37)

---

[5] K. Marx and F. Engels, *On Religion* (Moscow, 1957), p. 74 – the statement was made in 1847.

and is taken up by both Matthew (18:1–3) and Luke (9:46–48) – so it was widely diffused and widely accepted preaching about how a follower should view the issue of power. Here is Mark's text:

> Then they came to Capernaum. While Jesus was in the house, he asked them, 'What were you discussing on the way?' But they were silent, for on the way they had been arguing about which of them was the greatest. Sitting down, Jesus called the Twelve and said, 'If anyone wants to be first, he must be the last of all and the servant of all.' Then He had a little child stand among them. Taking the child in his arms, he said to them, 'Whoever welcomes one of these little children in my name welcomes me, and whoever welcomes me welcomes not only me, but the One who sent me.'
>
> Then James and John, the sons of Zebedee, came to Jesus and declared, 'Teacher, we want you to do for us whatever we ask.' 'What do you want me to do for you?' he inquired. They answered, 'Grant that one of us may sit at your right hand and the other at your left in your glory.' 'You do not know what you are asking,' Jesus replied. 'Can you drink the cup I will drink, or be baptised with the baptism I will undergo?' 'We can,' the brothers answered. 'You will drink the cup that I drink,' Jesus said, 'and you will be baptised with the baptism that I undergo. But to sit at my right or left is not mine to grant. These seats belong to those for whom they have been prepared.' When the ten heard about this, they became indignant with James and John. So Jesus called them together and said, 'You know that those regarded as rulers of the Gentiles lord it over them, and their superiors exercise authority over them. But it shall not be this way among you. Instead, whoever wants to become great among you must be your servant, and whoever wants to be first must be the slave of all. For even the Son of Man did not come to be served, but to serve, and to give his life as a ransom for many.'

The inversion of power is not simply *an* idea, but *the* idea about disciples' behaviour. The whole group is identified as being susceptible to this form of failure to take on board the message of Jesus, and this device is the evangelist's way of showing that it can corrupt the whole community of disciples. This revolution in how we relate to one another affects our relationship with God, our state 'in glory' and how we perceive the suffering of Jesus.

While neither Matthew nor Luke have such an extensive incident to make this point, both repeat the key memory: 'whoever humbles himself like this child, he is the greatest in the kingdom of heaven' (Matt 18:1–3); and 'he who is least among you all is the one who is great' (Luke 9:46–48). While the communities were clearly failing in this (we know this because they were arguing over power), the inversion was their counter-cultural vision which they believed they had to hand on as a key to their identity.

The theme is also found Matthew 20:1–16 – the parable of the vineyard owner who paid the same wages to three groups irrespective of whether they had worked for a whole day, parts of it, or barely at all – which still today provokes outrage when read because it is so unjust in our economic terms. But the purpose of this kind of story is to provoke reaction so that we are shocked by its main point: the values of the kingdom are not those of the surrounding society. Matthew then makes, again, his key point: 'So the last will be first, and the first will be last.'

In Mark 10:35–45 we have a repeat of the story we have just read from Mark 9. The same characters are seeking places at either hand of Jesus in glory, and once again Jesus tells them that they must be prepared to drink from his cup, before ending up with the key message:

> You know that those regarded as rulers of the Gentiles lord it over them, and their superiors exercise authority over them. But it shall not be this way among you. Instead, whoever wants to become great among you must be your servant, and whoever wants to be first must be the slave of all. For even the Son of Man did not come to be served, but to serve, and to give his life as a ransom for many.

This is one of the so-called 'doublet texts' where scholars speculate as to why such repetitions occur. Rather than see such duplications as literary blunders in transmission, when we recall that these texts are literary records of oral performances we can come to a simpler explanation: repetition in oral performances serves to drive home the message. Matthew seems to have learned from this repetition because he draws out in detail this message in his version (Matt 20:20–28) and in even more pointed language: 'the great one must be your servant, and first among you must be your slave'.[6]

---

6. It is this verse (Matt 20:27), combined with Gen 9:25, in their Latin forms that gives rise to the Bishop of Rome's title of 'Servant of the Servants of

However, in terms of a dramatic exposition of the theme, John's gospel is probably trumps. Here it is not only a matter of Jesus's words, but of his actions which he then tells the disciples should be paradigmatic for interaction between themselves. Set at the climax of Jesus' ministry, the final supper in Jerusalem before his arrest, crucifixion and death, Jesus washes the feet of those at table with him (John 13:1–16).[7] Washing the feet of guests before a meal was a common element in elite hospitality in the ancient world. Guests having come over mucky, none too clean, streets would have welcomed the chance to 'clean up' before they lay on a couch for a formal evening meal; and, indeed, many gathering for the Christian meal might have wanted just such an opportunity so that they could relax and eat the meal without the sense that they had the dirt and detritus of the street on their feet. However, and this is the key point, if this service was being performed by a host for his guests, then the actual task of washing the feet fell to the lowliest female slave in the household.

In washing the feet of the assembly – those at table with him – Jesus was not setting out some quaint little drama of humility such as it has become in later Christian liturgy, but taking on a role all present would have understood only too well. Jesus was breaking not only the power pyramid, but the gender pyramid. He was taking on a female role – in a male-dominated society; a slave's role – in a stratified slave-owning society; and the role of the servant – in a social setting where precedence and rank was a central concern. Yet the bottom line of this incident in John's narrative comes to us as if we had never heard it:

> If I then, the Lord and the Teacher, washed your feet, you also ought to wash one another's feet. For I gave you an example that you also should do as I did to you. (John 13:14–15)

Have you taken part in a mutual foot washing as a way of demonstrating that you understand the core dynamic of discipleship?[8]

God' (*Servus servorum Dei*). The Latin reads: *qui voluerit inter vos primus* (first among you) *esse erit vester servus* (your slave).

7. T. O'Loughlin, *Washing Feet: Imitating the Example of Jesus in the Liturgy Today* (Collegeville, MN, 2015).

8. T. O'Loughlin, 'From a Damp Floor to a New Vision of Church: Footwashing as a Challenge to Liturgy and Discipleship', *Worship*, 88 (2014), pp. 137–50.

Figure 14. The servant of the servants – and do not forget it!
Pope Sixtus V 'reigned' – note the verb – as pope from 1585-90.
This statue in the Italian city of Loreto presents a ruler determined
to show his significance to, and power over, his 'subjects.' A power
– note the vestments – that is imagined to derive from his being
a disciple of Jesus. The colossal scale of the image can be gauged
from the sitting figures nearby.

Pyramid Structures

Given the fact that power pyramids are everywhere within human society – and there are even pecking orders within the other species of primates such as the 'silverback' leading males within troops of gorillas – it would appear that this is the part of discipleship that is least in contact with human (or even primate) reality. What is even more surprising, this juxtaposition with human experience was not some gradually evolving religious idea that crept up on the Christian message over centuries so that the final outcome – however bizarre – could be explained by a long series of small steps (or missteps) and ever more complicated deductions. The radical confrontation of the vision of relationships proposed in Jesus' name by his early followers was *ab initio* at odds with society and even their own practice. Can this be explained?

There is no satisfactory way of accounting for this except in terms of Jesus' own conception of our relationship with God. The very otherness of the Creator (who is beyond creation) who is also intimate to all as Creator (who holds all in existence) is mirrored in the otherness of the manner of relating to one another. If each is loved uniquely and totally – and so equally – by the God who shows no partiality (cf. Rom 2:10), then the summit of discipleship is that we love each other in some manner that reflects the divine love for us.

The embedding of discipleship within life now ceases to something that can either be ignored as an ideal or is a goal to be attained by stringent effort, rather it must be embedded within our consciousness. Then, just as 'God is always more' (*Deus semper maior*) is a constant reminder that we do not comprehend the divine, so the call to be least of all and servant of all is the constant reminder that discipleship is never complete.

Ministry as Facilitation

What then is the most basic element of ministry? While most Christian discussion of ministry takes the form of a discussion of functions within the church – such as the role of the preacher, the presbyter, or of a healer – this must be secondary to the call to relate to each other in this most Christ-like way. The fundamental ministry is that of helping the other along the path of life. Service is all the practical tasks set out in Matthew's preaching as feeding, clothing, visiting – and only when these actual needs are met can we begin to talk about the very specialist 'religious' ministries. We as incomplete and needy human beings should have our lives made easier for us by the fact that there are disciples of Jesus, and as disciples of Jesus we should be making life easier for those around us.

This priority of the practical is itself counter-intuitive in terms of religious discourse: surely it is the preaching of the message, the formulation of the religious imagination, and the attention to the sacred that has primacy? Moral actions and practice would/should then follow as consequences of that religious engagement? This might be true at the level of knowing or of theological abstraction, but within discipleship it is actual service to our sisters and brothers in need that has primacy. This is neither top-down nor bottom-up; it is a mutuality of service that gives expression to the mutuality of love.

This primacy of the 'horizontal' (i.e. service to other humans) over the 'vertical' (i.e. service/worship of God in religious activities) has been a debated point within many churches for much of the twentieth century. The usual 'solution' is to engage in a rhetorical display aimed at avoiding the issue: 'it is not an "either/or" but a "both/and"'. Or some game of images: 'you cannot move sideways without moving upwards and you cannot move upwards without moving sideways'. Such fudges may make preachers feel that they have squared the circle, but in so doing they have missed the point. Christianity is distinctive in that it places the service of the neighbour – the one in actual, tangible, and proximate need – firmly in the first place. In an ideal world all would be balanced, but in the messy reality in which we live, we serve the needy first. When that is done, when the crisis is past, when the pain is relieved and the pangs of hunger are gone, then there will be time for formal prayer, lovely liturgy, and reflections on the truth of the gospel. But right now, there may be more urgent matters – a sister or brother suffering – and discipleship is about serving that person.

It is from this perspective that we can set out to read familiar texts not simply as moral guidelines but as touching this central element in discipleship. Luke's parable of 'the Good Samaritan' (Luke 10:25–37) seems to address how the desire for 'eternal life' – the question posed to Jesus is: 'what shall I do to inherit eternal life', which is a variant on 'how do I become a beneficiary of the covenant' – elicits the clarification that caring for one's neighbour in the happenstance of need is the safest guide to discipleship. Not only does the parable close with the instruction 'Go and do likewise', but the audience is invited to note that the boundaries of religious propriety are seen as irrelevant to the fulfilment of the covenant in comparison with the actual need. This is similar to the statement found in 1 John 4:20: it is the actual person that you can see that has the priority over the abstract statement of love for God. In that early text it is placed as the key soundbite within a homily:

> Whoever claims to love God yet hates a brother or sister is a liar. For whoever does not love their brother and sister, whom they have seen, cannot love God, whom they have not seen.

This saying again highlights the everyday nature of the encounters by which discipleship is expressed.

Ministry to the World

If this ministry to others in need occurs, quite literally as we see in the parable, as we wander along the road on our everyday business, it affects the notion of the sphere of ministry in ways that many Christians find difficult to imagine. Ministry is not an 'in church' activity, despite the fact that this is what the word ministry calls to mind either exclusively or almost exclusively. Ministry is the generic name of the set of activities of each disciple as they go about their everyday lives – and it is against that criterion that they need to assess their own discipleship. Discipleship involves taking a responsibility to the whole of humanity – indeed the whole of the creation – so that the path of each is made easier by the encounter. It seeks to give service to the world with the same generosity that God gives his love to the world and it is exemplified in the statement that 'the Son of Man did not come to be served, but to serve, and to give his life as a ransom for many' (Mark 9:37).

So how can we describe the basic activity of the community of disciples, the church? The church is those who, having a vision of the loving nature of God, seek in the occasions of their everyday lives to care for and love their neighbours. Everything else that is said about it is secondary.

Who Ministers What to Whom?

One stable of Christian publishing is books on ministry, which range from training manuals to theological justifications of the various disputes between the churches on the powers and authorities of their various officers. Most start with the fact of there being specific ministries – e.g.

a presbyter – and then relate the call of Jesus that the leader should be the servant of all to this being a characteristic of that office. The office comes first, the challenge relates to the style in which the office is exercised. The basic fact is that there is 'a priest' – duly ordained and with clear expectations about what she/he does in relation to others. That activity is the priest's 'ministry'. Then, the style of that ministry is considered: it should be done in a spirit of humble service so that, ideally, it is characterised by 'service' rather than a relationship of power. This sequence even takes on a liturgical form in many Christian assemblies at Easter. The parish priest on Holy Thursday presents himself/herself in the role of Jesus vis-à-vis the disciples and then washes the feet of a few in the congregation: the message is that the priest serves them with humility. The relationship of priest to congregation is what is primary, the notion of service is a qualifier on that relationship and sets out what is claimed as the nature of the ministry. The action of the priest showing top-down humility obscures the actual text of the gospel and its call that *all the disciples* (everyone in the gathering) should be washing one another's feet. Everyone serving everyone. However, this sequence of formal ministry then discipleship – hallowed by nearly two millennia of those in authority in the churches expounding their vision of themselves to other Christians – is precisely the vision of authority that our early texts on discipleship contradict.

The fundamental ministry is that of all the baptised to one another and to the human community. Every more specific form of ministry, from that of the man who is responsible for opening the church-hall on Sunday morning and making sure to the heating is turned on to that of Patriarch of Constantinople or Archbishop of Canterbury must be viewed as merely a consequence of this. So how should we relate such specific forms of ministry to discipleship? It is now time to examine in detail how discipleship forms the context for formal ministry rather that the reverse.

Chapter 8

The Shapes of Ministry

Skills for the Community

Meet any group of Christians and mention discipleship and, within minutes, the topic will mutate to a discussion of the specialist forms of formal 'ministry'. The actual content of the discussion will vary with the make-up of the group. With Orthodox Christians it will often focus on the topic of monasticism and how the monastery relates to the larger ecclesiastical set-up. With Roman Catholics the focus will be on the 'priestly' ministry of the clergy versus the role of the rest of the baptised within the church. Within the reformed churches the debate tends to focus on how formal ministry should be structured to reflect that church's self-understanding. Indeed, some of the most bitter disputes historically and today are over structural issues relating to ministry. Moreover, the questions relating to these formal ministries often replace the more fundamental issues of discipleship.

However, this leaves us with some problems. First, anyone seeking to approach the issue of discipleship in a Christian community today needs to come to some view on the nature of that community's formal ministry. Ministry may be secondary to discipleship, but one cannot think about discipleship without giving some thought to a church's formalised ministries. Second, while many churches make elaborate claims for their ministries being derived from the direct will of the Christ, we have to view all such claims as historically valueless. There is no evidence Jesus gave any thought to having specifically skilled people among his followers.[1] Furthermore, and just as importantly, while we soon find people with specific titles in the communities that look back to Jesus, it is only by appeals to notions of 'development' that any link can be made between those early individuals and the office-holders claiming special sacral powers that we find in third and fourth centuries. Third, while it is tempting to study how specifically named groups – such as 'the presbyters' – operated in the early churches, we do not get sufficient detailed information to give us more than the fact that there were people with that designation in some of the churches: so a study of formalised ministry that addresses our experience cannot be derived from early texts.[2] Fourth, we have issues today – such as gender equality within church structures – that we must address, but which could only be related to early texts by a gross anachronism. This chasm between 'the origins' and the claims of those who are 'ordained', a notion derived from Roman social organisation in the later empire, is threatening to most Orthodox and Roman Catholic Christians – along with some from the churches of the Reformation – but it is better to face this chasm than to engage in polemics as if Jesus thought in terms of hierarchy which transmitted its sacral powers to a specially selected core group within the community of the baptised.

Skilled Ministry

At first sight, the issue of 'ministry' would appear to be simple. Every religion, and every Christian denomination, has religious leaders, and these take the leading roles at its rituals. Thus we talk about 'priests' in various religions, and even in a religion like Islam where the term has no strict meaning, we still speak about 'Muslim clerics'. Moreover, ritual requires expertise, and the amount of expertise required is usually a direct function of the length of the group's remembered tradition: these experts, nowadays usually formally trained, are its office-holders and liturgical ministers. Thus a presbyter in an Eastern Orthodox church needs to know about a complex ritual harbouring elements that have grown up over a period of perhaps 1,700 years; while the leader of a contemporary western evangelical church, while eschewing any inherently sacral status, still needs to claim special expertise as a biblical teacher. For

---

[1.] Avis, 'The Paschal Mystery and the Church'.

[2.] S. Laeuchli, *Power and Sexuality: The Emergence of Canon at the Synod of Elvira* (Philadelphia, 1972).

Figure 15. Ministry is ... helping in a foodbank.
The action of sharing food with the needy is part of 'the public service'
(literally: 'liturgy') of disciples. While it does not take place in a 'sacred place,'
nor is it flagged as a 'religious' activity, it forms the basis of all Christian
worship, which is service to God and neighbour – especially the poor.

Roman Catholics, they deem seven years of 'formation' followed by a
life of celibacy as necessary. Such expertise is then seen as the empirical
basis for ministry (either in parallel with or apart from some notion of
authorisation such as 'ordination'), and then those experts 'minister to'
the other church members, by carrying out the rituals, leading the group
in its liturgies, or acting as its teachers during worship. In each case there
is a binary model at work: a sole minister or small ministry-group which
acts, leads, and preaches/speaks/teaches on one side, and opposite them a
much larger group which attends/listens/receives ministry.

We see this model in a nutshell in the phrase: 'the clergy administer the
sacraments'. This is a valuable and widely appreciated model because it fits
well beside other expert service providers in society (e.g. medics providing
healthcare to the rest of the community or accountants providing financial
services), and, therefore, full-time 'ministers of religion' are aligned
by society, and often by themselves, with those other experts. Indeed,
trained ministers do have a great deal of expertise, honed by experience,
in comparison with most other church members, and this, coupled with

a service ethos, thrusts them into leadership positions such that ministry takes on the shape of 'active' giving by leaders, while the rest are 'passive' receivers. The dynamics of ministry in the liturgical space are not unlike the dynamic of actors/audience in a theatre: each is participating, one group by giving a performance, the other by receiving and responding to it. Moreover, in society many tasks are carried out on behalf of the whole group by a specialist cadre (e.g. politics or policing) and the small group acts with deputed authority; and a religious variant of this can be found in the notion of a 'priesthood'/a 'clergy' in many religions which have a specialist temple personnel (e.g. the Levites in ancient Jerusalem). Thus, because society needs a 'chaplaincy' service, we can easily imagine that this is the justification for having clergy (whether or not such a group's existence is compatible with the basic inspiration of the Christian ministry which views each of the baptised as a minister). This kind of justification for ministry is now rarely proposed by Christians living in multicultural situations, but it was widely used when they imagined their societies as homogeneously Christian or Catholic – and it is still far more influential both among those who reject the Church and those who pine for a lost era of church-centrality than is often recognised.

Discipleship as Community Service

In stark contrast to such highly structured notions of ministry or priesthoods, Christians have the memories of the first disciples of Jesus. Jesus was not a Levite, his ministry barely engaged with the formal religious expert systems, and when those structures are recalled (e.g. Luke 10 31 and 32; John 4:21), they are the objects of criticism or presented as transient. Moreover, while Jesus was presented as appointing messengers/preachers (apostles) there is no suggestion that these were thought of as ritual experts. Although leaders emerged in the various early churches (with a variety of names: e.g. 'elders', *presbuteroi*, or 'overseer-servants', *episkopoi kai diakonoi*, originally a double-name for a single person, but which later on would divide into two ranks: 'bishop' and 'deacon'), it took generations (until the later second century – contradicting older textbooks we know now that Ignatius of Antioch wrote after 160 *at the earliest*) for those patterns to be harmonised between communities and then systematised into authority structures. There is no suggestion in the first-century documents that leadership at the two key community events, baptism and eucharist, was restricted in any way or the preserve of those who were community leaders, much less a specially authorised group. The link between (a) leadership of the community and (b) presidency at the eucharistic meal (a linkage that would drive much later thinking on ministry and even today is a major source of Christian division) would not be forged until the third century, and only later again would 'the history of its institution' by Jesus be constructed. Even more explicit was the remembered teaching upon leadership in the community where there was to be radical equality among church members, for example in this story:

> And Jesus ... said to them, 'You know that those who are supposed to rule over the Gentiles lord it over them, and their great men exercise authority over them. But it shall not be so among you; but whoever would be great among you must be your servant, and whoever would be first among you must be slave of all.' (Mark 10: 42–44)

This vision of equality is also found in the third 'do this' story in the gospels (the other 'do this' commands relate to baptism and the eucharist) in John 13:3–15 where the relationship of leaders in the community is modelled on that of washing the diners' feet by Jesus (as we have already noted, this was a task normally done by the lowest rank of female slave). Significantly, this action, despite the injunction in John 13:15, did not develop into a regular community practice! The followers of Jesus were to be (in two early second-century documents) a 'priestly people' (1 Pet 2:9: 'a priestly kingdom', *basileion hierateuma*) where all shared by baptism in Christ who was uniquely their priest (*hiereus*) (Heb 2:17). The notion of a distinct priestly group – a 'priesthood' in the strict sense of those with specific ritual powers – is wholly alien to the early vision. While many churches today do adopt this notion and are quite happy to refer to themselves as a 'priesthood' (a *sacerdotium*), they should note that their understanding owes more to them being substitutes for the civic priesthoods of the Graeco-Roman world than to the milieu of the first followers of Jesus – a fact witnessed in their occasional use of pagan terminology such as words like 'pontiff'/'pontifical' derived from 'the pontifices' who formed a specific ancient Roman priesthood.

The Church within Society

This tension between the empirical need for organisation within groups, coupled with the fact that power tends to concentrate and to be seen as a sacral faculty – a development facilitated by using a combination of Old Testament models and terminology and cultural assumptions taken from Graeco-Roman culture: e.g. *pontifex* or *ordo*), on the one hand, and the memory of what distinguishes the new priestly people in Christ where ministry was both more embracing (the whole community is the minister) and less structured (each can potentially take on any service for the others) can be seen as underlying all the later disputes about ministry and priesthood. Those disputes – and they still continue for many Christians – were made all the more intractable by the conviction on each side, in each dispute, that an explicit answer could be derived from their authoritative foundational sources!

It has long been an illusion of the various Christian denominations that a study of history – and particularly the first couple of centuries or the texts from those times they held to belong to the New Testament canon – could provide either a blueprint for ministry (e.g. 'the threefold structure of order': bishop, presbyter, deacon) or a conclusive answer to issues relating to ministry that have arisen in later situations (e.g. what 'power' can be seen as coming from Christ to the priest at the time of the Reformation, or can a woman preside at the eucharist today). This is an illusory quest for not only does it fall victim to the anachronism inherent in all appeals to a perfect original moment, an imagined period in the past when all was revealed (at least *in nuce*); but it assumes that ministry as it later developed was not itself the outcome of multiple, often conflicting, forces in the particular societies, as well as adaptations by Christians to well-known inherited religious structures. For example, the clerical system, within which liturgical ministry was/is located for much of Christian history, related originally to the political needs of the church as a public body within the Roman Empire. As that imperial society had highly organised priesthoods, so people took it for granted that similar groups would exist in the church. Likewise, the monastic elements that became linked with liturgical ministry resulted from the place of monasticism as the ideal of holiness in late antiquity; while the notion of 'hierarchy' (i.e. sacred power descends through intermediaries from higher to lower levels of reality: such that the holier leader, the 'hierarch', offers sacrifice 'on behalf of' or performs liturgy *for the others* as an effect of his special election and superior powers) fits Christian theology within a Neoplatonic worldview in a rigidly layered social environment.

Given that there was no 'original' plan for 'professional' ministry in the church, and as a result of centuries of disputes there are many conflicting views about what constitutes someone within ministry, it is quite impossible – except within the mythic spaces of particular denominations – to produce a systematic basis for liturgical ministry. However, given that ministry occurs and is needed, one can set out some criteria that can help individuals and communities to develop a pragmatic theology of liturgical ministry.

Criteria for Ministry

A balanced approach, both in practice and theologically, needs to take account of several factors.

a. Any Specific Ministry is a Variation on Baptismal Belonging

First, every specific ministry is a particular variation of the ministry of all the baptised, and in baptism there is a radical equality: 'there is neither Jew nor Greek, there is neither slave nor free, there is neither male nor female; for you are all one in Christ Jesus' (Gal 3:28). This radical equality is a characteristic of the new creation brought about in Christ; therefore, any subsequent distinctions such that particular ministries are not potentially open to every baptised person are tantamount to a defective theology of baptism by which all ministry is brought into being. It is baptism that constitutes the people who manifest the work of the Christ in the world.

Therefore, making further demands for 'signs' of particular divine election (e.g. being able to speak in tongues or handle snakes) as indications of suitability for ministry fly in the face of the incarnational dispensation seen in baptism. Likewise, regulations that restrict ministry to particular states of life (e.g. demanding celibacy as a condition for the presbyterate in the Roman Catholic church or for the episcopate in the Orthodox churches) have to be seen as a undue concern with the status of certain ministries, implying that baptism is merely some basic entry requirement for 'Christianity' rather than that which creates the new person who can minister, and in that new creation no such distinctions exist. Similarly, the notion that women, as such, can be excluded from ministry on the basis of some pragmatic historical appeal (e.g. 'Jesus did not ordain women!' – assuming such a pre-critical view of 'history' has any value) fails to take account of the fundamental role of baptism in all Christian existence and action. The slogan 'if you cannot ordain 'em, you shouldn't baptise 'em' may seem crude, but it does capture the fundamental insight that incorporation into the risen Christ (i.e. baptism) is the source of all liturgical ministry and of every particular act of liturgy.

b. All Ministry is Christ-ian

Second, it must respect the awareness that all action and ministry by Christians is *Christ*-ian in nature. Christians form a people, they are not simply a collection of individuals, and this is a priestly people because it acts in union with its unique High Priest, Jesus. It is the work of the Christ in blessing the Father that constitutes the reality of liturgy of the New Covenant, and the worship of the disciples is only *Christ*-ian liturgy in so far as it is through, with, and in Jesus. Individuals do not offer praise and petition except as part of the community, and the community only does so in so far as it acts in Christ. This fundamental dynamic becomes actual in the liturgy of particular gatherings. It is as a church, a real community, that we gather to celebrate our common meal of thanksgiving, and it is the church which blesses the Father. This desire of the assembly is given voice by the one presiding within the community, and this prayer of thanksgiving is made in, with, and through Jesus who makes us his people in the presence of the Father.

We all too often, and too easily, lose sight of the fact that Christians must think of their liturgy in a way that is radically opposed to that commonly found in other religions of a 'religious service' due to God or the gods. In that paradigm, the divine is the opposite of the world in which we live and to which something is owed, presented, transferred, and this constitutes a mode of contact with the divine realm which might constitute a debt of loyalty / praise/petition or appeasement. Making this connection, whether by an individual or a group, assumes a technical knowledge and some sacred skill – usually the work of a special priesthood – such that the divine recognises that the action performed is the appropriate sacred deed. Christians, contrariwise, conceive their worship on the basis that their priest has come to them and is with them as a community. Therefore, where two or three are gathered in the name of Jesus, he is with them (Matt 18:20), and so their actions together – such as celebrating a meal – take place in the presence of the Father, because Christ, present among them, is always their High Priest. This theological vision has important implications for individual Christians who find themselves performing specific acts, ministries, within the church.

First, professional Christian 'ministers' need to remember that, although in common perceptions they will be seen as the 'religious service experts' and as yet another variant of the religious phenomenon of 'priests' (a word designating sacred functionaries in most world religions – and studied as such in religious studies), this is not a good starting point for their own self-understanding. Christian history has too much distracting baggage resulting from its ministers taking over their understanding of their role within the church by analogy with the role of priests (*sacerdotes*), temples, and sacrifice in both the Old Testament and Graeco-Roman religions. Within Christianity, the ministry is that of the whole community – and so for that matter every Christian can, and perhaps should, own the designation 'minister of religion' – the difference between any two Christians (even if one has the most gaudy liturgical wardrobe and uniform, while the other wears none) is only a matter of external perception, accepted learned skills, and designated functions within the community. Secondly, it is worth remembering that language plays us false in understanding 'priestly ministry' in particular. In the Old Testament the *cohen* (which we render by the word 'priest') performed special tasks – as a matter of divine appointment – on behalf of the rest of Israel (see Leviticus and Numbers). This was rendered in the Septuagint by the word *hiereus* – a word commonly used for pagan temple officials – and then, later, into Latin by *sacerdos* which was a generic word covering all the various special temple 'priesthoods' such as *flamenes* and *pontifices*. The early Christians did not use these words for their leaders: *hiereus*/*sacerdos* belonged to Jesus alone in the heavenly temple. Christian leaders were designated *by their relation to the community*: as the one who oversaw, led, or served it. Later, the *hiereus*/*sacerdos* language was absorbed and became the basis of Christians' perceptions of their presbyters. So our word 'priest' is etymologically from the word *presbyter*, but conceptually it relates to the sacerdotal functions. One consequence of this is that those so designated think of themselves as 'ministers of God' – they perform a service to him – but it is the community in Christ that is the minister of God, and specific individual functionaries, such as presbyters, are ministers to the community. Thirdly, another consequence of Christian officials taking over a sacerdotal self-understanding was they explained their work (by parallel with Old Testament *cohenim*) in terms of its distinctiveness from that of the rest of the baptised, or as did pagan priesthoods (*sacerdotia*) as being specialists acting on behalf of ordinary people. Once this had occurred they had to ask what made them different and what special religious quality did they have which others did not possess: the answer came with the notion of a power 'to consecrate', and then this power (itself the subject of rhetorical inflation) became the basis of 'ontological difference' between them and 'ordinary Christians', or between their 'ordained priesthood' and a nebulous, and often ignored, 'common priesthood'. Not only is this 'priesthood defined by difference' theologically flawed, but it obscures the unique role of the Christ in Christian liturgy, it downplays the role of the church as 'the people of God', and it creates a 'two-tier' Christianity of the special religious people (e.g. clergy/monks/nuns) and passive 'other ranks' whose ministry is 'praying, paying, and obeying'.

After more than a millennium and a half of these confusions in Christianity, both east and west, it is very hard for many who see themselves as 'ministers' in a church – especially those with elaborate sacerdotal liturgies – to break free of this baggage. But for all its complex, gilded splendour, it is still a distracting deviation from core Christian beliefs. Meanwhile, some churches continue to evolve in its wake (e.g. the repeated declarations by the Catholic Church that women are absolutely excluded from the presbyterate[3]), while being conceptually cognisant of the problems of imaging ministry in terms of a distinct *sacerdotium*. Tradition can be like a great oil-tanker turning at sea: it takes a long time to overcome inertia, and for the ship to answer the helm!

c. Ministry is Actual Service Not Potency

Third, one of the thorniest questions that beset discussions, particularly between denominations, about ministry concerns the issue of authorisation. This usually presents as a discussion about 'ordination' within a sacerdotal model of 'priesthood' such as we have just examined. In such a model the priest must be thought of in terms of some specific 'power' and since this, unlike that of the Levites, does not come with birth, it must come from a specific act of empowerment: 'ordination'. Ordination, in turn, comes to be seen as an act of 'making something'. In such a situation a person is either 'the thing made', or not. So discussions between churches either ignore the issue (which renders the discussion little more than polite window dressing) or search to validate each other's 'orders' (which becomes a matter of arcane history and black/white answers). Such starting points only promote deadlock.

A far better approach is to note that all groups need, at least, some formal organisation, while Christians must also work with one another in communities (they claim to be called to love one another), and then to treat each such community as a basic church. Next, enquire if the ministry structures are adequate to helping them to pray together, to receive teaching that promotes understanding and discipleship, to keep them together as a group, to answer specific needs a group might have

---

3. This was explicitly made by Pope John Paul II in his encyclical *Ordinatio sacerdotalis* of 1994; it was followed by other Vatican statements in, e.g., 1995, 1998, 2002, and 2008, and in 2016 Pope Francis declared it a closed issue citing the statements of his two predecessors.

Figure 16. Clearly religious: a Roman altar.
This is a *domestic* religious artefact – an altar set up in a pre-Christian
household that commemorates a dead wife. Much of the language used
by Christians for the own worship and structures (e.g. 'altar' or
'ordination') owes more to Greco-Roman cultural values than the
images of discipleship found in the gospels.

(e.g. poor, old, young families), and ensure that the ministers do not
behave in a manner that is tyrannical (as can happen all too easily in
ministry) or abusive (it is easy for 'religious authorities' to take advantage
of the trust given them), or self-serving (a problem already noted in the
mid-first century). Whoever fulfils these needs and functions should
be seen as 'the ministers' of that community, and respected as such by
other churches and groups of ministers. The differences in the styles and
structures can be considered subsequently as part of the varied tapestry
of the work of the Spirit and historical circumstances – and they can
learn from one another which elements from the others' visions of
ministry they might import – and which of their own they need to
change or drop!

d. Service Requires Skills
Fourth, most specific expressions of ministry to the community require
some level of skill and this, given the way humans develop, will come
from ability, experience, and training. Many churches are not far beyond

the older position whereby if one passed an academic course in theology or was deemed 'fit for orders', then training in liturgical ministry was but a practical afterthought. In traditional societies where 'going to church' was part of the week, few cared whether or not a minister had any sensitivity to leading people in liturgy. However, an adequate view of liturgy, and the nature of contemporary Christian belonging, requires far more awareness of the skills needed for this ministry. Thus, someone presiding at the eucharist needs to have the skills of a host at a great celebratory meal; and if that is a task that fills them with dread (note the number who fear such roles at weddings, for example), then that person should not be called on to preside and give voice to the community. Likewise, someone who dislikes public speaking or lacks aptitude as a teacher will find preaching difficult – and this cannot be remedied by training in 'communication skills'. A basic ministry skill in most communities today is the ability to lead spontaneous prayer – which needs great sensitivity and some of the art of the poet – so someone who lacks this skill is not someone who, simply in virtue of ordination, should presume to be able to lead a community in its prayer. By contrast, those who are good communicators are often poor listeners, and so they will not be so good in ministries of reconciliation. And while we can all benefit from growing in sensitivity for those who are suffering, a ministry of healing will fit best with someone with 'a bedside manner'. We should see the Spirit empowering each community with the variety of skills it needs, and then aligning each individual's skill to the necessary tasks as the work of ecclesial vocation. After such alignment, formal training (always valuable given the haphazard way humans absorb information) is a case of organising, developing, and drawing out charisms latent in the individual as a member of the community. Rituals like ordination should be seen as actualising and recognising gifts already within the church from the work of the Spirit, rather than the conferring of 'powers' extrinsic to the person.

Moreover, liturgical ministry is *not* a matter of holes and pegs. Rather, it is a community recognising its needs in Christ, and of individuals deploying, creatively, their range of gifts, insights, and skills (a mix unique to each person) in the service of their church. Each liturgical ministry should actualise that person's distinctive contribution to a unique moment in Christian history. Liturgical ministry is an art as much as a skill or a 'vocation'.

The standard one-size-fits-all model of the cleric (usually chosen for other criteria than liturgical ministry) who in virtue of 'ordination' carries out every ministry cannot be justified either theologically (for it ignores the Spirit's workings in an actual church) nor practically, as no individual can be presumed to have that skill-range nor be able to deploy such adaptability on a day-to-day basis. A deeper awareness of the needs of liturgical ministry leads to basic questioning of most ministry training models – many denominations are still too content with that of 'the one-person show' – and this is a major challenge facing churches today.

e. Ministry is Not Equivalent to Management

Fifth, churches grow, and often become vast international organisations with consequent management needs. Down the centuries these larger bodies have often assumed that those initially chosen for their skill in liturgical ministry would automatically have management ability (at least at local levels), and, conversely, it has always been assumed that those with the widest administrative duties (e.g. bishops, popes, patriarchs) would be the most senior and capable liturgical ministers – and sometimes this has been the case! However, just as there are varieties of skills within liturgical ministry, so liturgy as the *Christ*-ian expression of the community is different from church management, and, consequently, there is a difference in the abilities needed between those who perform specific tasks in each sphere. In those churches with highly structured line-management, it is often the case that the leaders, usually bishops 'with the power of jurisdiction', are also expected to be able to take the lead in liturgy – and this is not a problem if liturgy is seen just as a derivative of 'the power of order'. However, experience often shows that such managers (and such are needed) are not those who can either teach adequately or lead worship effectively; and the converse situations are also true: a good academic or a sensitive pastor of a small community may turn out to be a useless bishop. A deeper consciousness of such problems – and they come to light most clearly when we consider professional ministry – inevitably leads to an awareness of the need in most churches for them to consider afresh the whole set of interlocking structures that come with bounds of 'church ministry'.

Where do we Start?

In every community there are those who have the skills that have brought that group together and given it an identity. This, in ecclesial terms, reflects the silent working of the Spirit gathering the scattered individuals and transforming them into the body of the Christ. The task is to recognise these actual ministers and to facilitate them to make that ministry more effective and fruitful. Some will have the gifts of evangelising and welcoming, others the skills of leading in prayer and the offering of the thanksgiving sacrifice of praise, others the gifts of teaching, others of reconciling, others for the mission of each community to the building up of the kingdom of justice and peace, and some will have the management skills to pay the bills. None is greater and none is less – a shocking idea to many in the highly clerical churches but no more than the Johannine vision of mutual ministry set in the climactic moment of the Last Supper.

In every discussion of ministry we need to have the advice of Paul to the church in Corinth in 58 CE echoing in our heads as he presents ministry as the working out of the presence of the Spirit in the assembly:

> Now there are varieties of gifts, but the same Spirit; and there are varieties of services, but the same Lord; and there are varieties of activities, but it is the same God who activates all of them in everyone. To each is given the manifestation of the Spirit for the common good. To one is given through the Spirit the utterance of wisdom, and to another the utterance of knowledge according to the same Spirit, to another faith by the same Spirit, to another gifts of healing by the one Spirit, to another the working of miracles, to another prophecy, to another the discernment of spirits, to another various kinds of tongues, to another the interpretation of tongues.
>
> All these are activated by one and the same Spirit, who allots to each one individually just as the Spirit chooses. For just as the body is one and has many members, and all the members of the body, though many, are one body, so it is with Christ.
>
> For in the one Spirit we were all baptized into one body – Jews or Greeks, slaves or free – and we were all made to drink of one Spirit. (1 Cor 12:4–13)

Sometime later in the first century, when the followers of Jesus were coming to grips with the religious earthquake of the destruction of the Temple in Jerusalem, one of Paul's followers reframed that vision in terms of each ministry being the gift of the risen and ascended Christ present in each community:

The gifts he gave were that some would be apostles, some prophets, some evangelists, some pastors and teachers, to equip the saints for the work of ministry, for building up the body of Christ, until all of us come to the unity of the faith and of the knowledge of the Son of God, to maturity, to the measure of the full stature of Christ. (Eph 4:11–13)

If these statements reverberated through contemporary discussions we might talk less about 'closing churches' and 'the shortage of ministers' and could then move on to the more fruitful task of discovering the wealth of vocations that are all around us. While this is intolerable to all those churches who are committed to a full-time, professional 'priesthood' with a strong *esprit de corps* – such as the clergy have had in Roman Catholicism and in Orthodoxy since the fourth century – we might note that the future is rarely like the past; and when a present seeks to recede into its past, it is untrue to its own moment.

Moreover, to the extent that any group of Christians adopts the self-identity of being a community of disciples, the greater is the need to revision formal ministry as being just accidental expressions of the call given to each person who seeks to follow Jesus.

Chapter 9

Discipleship in the Future

Moving in Unchartered Waters

Christianity is a religion that is future focussed – we see this in images such as 'the kingdom of God' and the prayer 'thy kingdom come' – but one which also looks backwards to the community of Israel, to the time and events linked by believers to Jesus acclaimed by them as the Christ, and to the communities of his followers that sprang up round the Mediterranean world in the first centuries – and to some of their writings which have been given the status of 'scripture' and then read in common with such designations as 'the word of the Lord'. Indeed, it is hard to imagine any gathering of Christians at which some part of the scriptures is not read and, consequently, in which there is no evocation of the past.

But this link to the past is problematic in many ways. There is probably no other area of Christianity where there is such a range of opinions and as much confusion as about what is meant by 'the Bible' or how it relates to discipleship. For some, with only a superficial understanding of Christianity, 'the Bible' is virtually equivalent to the religion, We see this confusion in our cliché of referring to an essential text on any subject as 'the Bible of this or that'. Then there are those who claim that those writings are equivalent to the revelation of God: the answer to any question is, it seems, to be found by asking 'what does the Bible say?' To this group the hard question is this: can we take 'the Bible' as 'the Bible of Christianity'? For anyone who has read this far in this book, it will be clear that this is a position I consider untenable: neither were those texts written with a modern audience in mind, nor were they written as if they could provide a consistent guide to discipleship in their own time. 'Christianity' is not a worked-out philosophy, but the name applied as a religious description to a community that felt its way forwards confident that Jesus had opened for them a way to God as their loving Father.

Throughout this book we have been seeing in one context or another the haphazard way in which the message of Jesus within Second Temple Judaism was transformed as a new movement, heavily Gentile in membership, and became a distinct religion. A religion that looked back to its Jewish origins as little more than a backstory, and which acted within the Graeco-Roman world – and in a few places outside that world – as one more religious option. This shift, which would have been incomprehensible to Jesus and those around him, can be most quickly seen in the change in the groups' self-perception from seeing themselves at the end of history, a conclusion, to being the start-up of a whole new level of divine revelation, a beginning. The movement's inherited Jewish library moved from being *the* scriptures, to being prologue, to being simply 'old'.

The Jesus movement's own writings are almost devoid of plan and were put together as documents of the moment rather than as a manifesto or as ground-plan for a widespread movement. Moreover, diversity was present at every turn so that we cannot fit them into any overall pattern – although this has been a theological dream for centuries[1] – and the actual documents that have survived are only a fraction of those which were being read in the early assemblies. Luke opened his written gospel with an acknowledgement of this:

> Inasmuch as many have undertaken to compile a narrative of the things which have been accomplished among us, just as they were delivered to us by those who from the beginning were eyewitnesses and ministers of the word, it seemed good to me also, having followed all things closely for some time past, to write an orderly account for you, most excellent Theophilus, that you may know the truth concerning the things of which you have been informed. (1:1–4)

[1.] T. O'Loughlin, 'The *Protevangelium Jacobi* and the Emergence of the Notion of Consistency as a "Principle" within Christian Theology', in J.N. Bremmer, J. Andrew Doole, Thomas R. Karmann, Tobias Nicklas, and Boris Repschinski (eds.), *The Protevangelium of James* (Leuven, 2020), pp. 206–16.

How might our understanding of the disciples of the first century be changed if even a portion of these accounts – which many had undertaken – had survived: all we know is Mark's gospel and that there was a collection of sayings which we refer to, somewhat abstractly, as 'Q'.

But there is an even more pressing question: if all that material from the first century CE – including some verifiably verbatim quotes from Jesus himself – had survived, could we claim that it was still relevant in our world, now and in the future? This, as it turns out, is just a variation on the question of whether there is a plan for discipleship – a fixed agenda – or whether discipleship is open-ended and a matter of diligent discovery. The process is not one of 'looking up the answers' but seeking insights within a faith in a loving God that may provide a vision of a new society. Since discipleship's challenge will take a plethora of forms, what follows is not a plan, but a series of experiments in reflection and imagination.

The Challenge of Equality

Equality was not a significant issue either in the ancient world or for most of the period since then. The first Christians lived with slavery, many were slaves, and, at best, Christian teachers encouraged masters to treat their slaves with compassion. There is no evidence that Christians supported any revolt by slaves, but rather the contrary: the good order of society was a something to be prayed for and supported (Rom 13:1–8 and, later, 1 Tim 2:2). Inequality was a fact of life: every relationship articulated the subtle levels of the society and who was 'up' and who 'down'. Poverty was endemic and while there were obligations towards the poor, there was no emphasis on eradicating poverty as a systemic problem. It was just another fact of life and was even justified as inevitable by appeal to a statement in the gospels: 'the poor you have with you always' (Mark 14:7) – a classic case of how *not* to cite the Bible. Moreover, there were established 'values' within society that were accepted without question, and these often were the exact opposite of any notion of equality.[2] The most glaring example is that women are not equal to men within either society or the church, and this was supported by a bit of second-century thinking with scriptural status: 'And it was not Adam who was deceived; it was the woman who was deceived and became a sinner' (1 Tim 2:14).

---

[2] J.A. Glancy, *Slavery as Moral Problem: In the Early Church and Today* (Minneapolis, MN, 2011).

Figure 17. An *ikonostasis*: religion is about separation.
The notion of distinguishing the holy/unholy, sacred/profane, ordinary/
special is deeply embedded in many cultures and takes material forms in
Christian buildings. But does it accord with the teaching of Jesus or with
the confession that in Jesus the Logos has 'pitched his tent' – his
'tabernaculum' – in the midst of the creation?

Equally, that there was a hierarchy within human society was seen as a
rationale for hierarchy in the church – and since the time of the Pseudo-
Denis it was even seen as explaining why there is a hierarchy among the
angels. Equality did not even get a chance in heaven! Our contemporary
notion of equality came from Enlightenment thought and was even
seen as being opposed to the Christian religious vision. Indeed, some
of the most vehement opponents of the related values espoused by the
French Revolution of liberty, fraternity, and equality were the Christian
hierarchies.

Given this history we might be surprised that many churches now see
opposition to slavery as a central message of the gospel – and many, if not
most, Christians would without a hesitation say that this is the teaching
of Jesus. But Jesus – insofar as we can access his thought through the
early preaching within the churches – never addressed the issue! So
where did the certainty that his disciples today must reject slavery, and
(more contentiously) promote human equality, come from?

The awareness of what is demanded of the person of faith is an ever-expanding horizon. Just as our awareness in every other area of life increases, so can our understanding of the implications of the gospel. This is not an automatic progress such that 'in every age, in every way, the Church is getting better and better'. There are any number of cases where churches have 'developed' and the growth has been cancerous. The western church made a massive development in the sixth century with the notion that one could 'sponsor' – with money or food – a cleric to say masses that would have an assured effect on releasing souls from torment. The idea was an immediate success – especially when Pope Gregory the Great got behind it – and spread across western Europe. Not only did it reduce faith to commerce, it vitiated the centrality of love within discipleship, it contributed – after the best part of a 1,000 years – to the splitting up of the Latin church at the Reformation, and is still a distraction for some Roman Catholics. Likewise, the Orthodox churches became so fascinated by the 'otherness' of the holy mysteries that they lost sense of its being the communal meal of the baptised around a table. They ended up with a wall separating the table, where the clergy were located, and the rest of the building. Because the wall, the *ikonostasis*, was beautiful, no one asked the key question: does it not contradict how we are to assemble? Closer to our time, in the first half of the twentieth century the Dutch Reformed in South Africa reread such myths as that of the Tower of Babel (Gen 11:1–9) and, through this process, came up with a theological justification for Apartheid. It is a warning to us all that, when our society wants to force something, it can often use religion as a cover.

So what amounts to a genuine growth in our understanding of the call of faith in the loving God of Jesus affirmed as the Christ? Here is an early Christian rule of thumb:

> Finally, brothers [and sisters], whatever is true, whatever is honourable, whatever is just, whatever is pure, whatever is lovely, whatever is gracious, if there is any excellence, if there is anything worthy of praise, think about these things. (Phil 4:8–9)

We have to engage in continual reflection on what is needed: it requires conscientious judgement rather than 'looking it up' and then 'following the rules'. Presenting discipleship in the latter way not only cheapens it but betrays it. We have to ask 'what is best?' and then note the prompts that come from within us as to what is good, noble, and

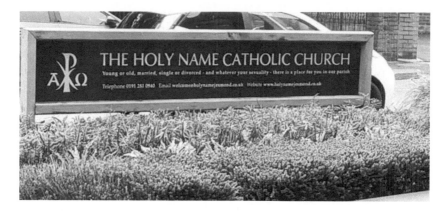

**Figure 18. Discipleship is about welcome – the sign outside a
church's building in Newcastle-upon-Tyne, England.**
For too many Christians the issue of LGBT+ is an open/shut one: 'they
must be excluded!' Indeed, this is the reaction most people expect from
churches! However, the welcoming of all into fellowship – manifesting
the divine love – is a fundamental demand of discipleship.

true. This process not only involves our human instincts for the good,
but requires trying to gain wisdom within the community of faith, and
prayer for enlightenment. The Christian holds that the Spirit lies within
each human being and can lead each of us to the truth, but, likewise, we
have to take account of human failings, weakness, and the fact that the
'still small voice' can be drowned out by the noise around us.

LGBT+

Equality – especially in its most simple forms such as the rejection of
slavery – is now a popular topic among Christians. One would find
very few – though they still exist with regard to gender equality – who
would argue for a full-blown hierarchical universe. There is a simple
way to see this shift in perspective: when was the last time you heard a
congregation sing 'All things bright and beautiful' and include this, very
nineteenth-century, verse: 'The rich man in his castle / the poor man at
his gate / God made them high and lowly / and ordered their estate'? But
there are other contemporary developments in our understanding of the
human person and the rights of individuals in society that are far more
contentious among some Christians.

Perhaps this is nowhere more common, worldwide, than in relation to the question of gay and lesbian followers of Jesus, and, more recently, those who are bisexual and trans.[3] Can they 'fit into' the household of God as disciples while respecting who they are as human beings? Here, it would seem, the Bible and the inherited tradition speak as one: this is an abomination! Whether or not one can find a verse here or there that might be more accommodating is irrelevant: the tradition of our society, written in broad strokes, is very clear in holding that any sexual expression other than that between a woman and a man is sinful, and should be considered a wilful act 'against the Law of God'. For the tradition it is black and white, and that is it! What does one do in this case when our human sense tells us that this denial of the variety of sexual orientations is wrong, and that we must respect the human rights of others, but 'the tradition' (understood as the legacy of the past rather than the activity of handing on from today to tomorrow) says the very opposite?

Here we face one of those tricky issues that Christian teachers have sought to avoid down the centuries: our religious resources may point us towards God, but they do not constitute a 'guide to the truth'. Thus any religious authority which claims such a total command of divine knowledge – and *all* churches have claimed this in the past at various times while they argued with one another as to what was the key to this treasure – is forgetting that, just as the biblical books took over Babylonian myths, and the Second Temple teachers and early Christians took over Platonic and Stoic thinking, and later theologians adapted Greek and Arab thinking, so today we need to draw in the skills of psychologists to help us in our quest for the good, the true, and the beautiful.

That said, what does one say to an archbishop in Africa who, when interviewed on a radio in 2021 confidently linked climate disasters, COVID-19, and homosexuality as 'God's judgement on wickedness'? Perhaps a place to start is by noting that there is a world of difference between someone, on the one hand, who claims to possess the truth, and, on the other, someone who claims to be seeking the truth. The second person is on a journey which is a common one with the journey of the disciple. For the Christian there is the vision of coming into the fullness of the truth with God 'at the end'; meanwhile we work with whatever fragments of truth we have, and thank God for human

---

[3] G. Loughlin (ed.), *Queer Theology: Rethinking the Western Body* (London, 2007).

wisdom and progress in knowing. Since we do not see the whole picture, we humbly move forward, always keeping in mind that gentleness, love, and tolerance must be our defaults. The confident archbishop may see himself as the spokesman for God, his religion, or the Bible, but he has probably not made the notion of a disciple on a journey central to his identity. Here lies the difference between discipleship and that seemingly related situation of church membership.

Does that mean that the Bible is just 'old hat'? To value the scriptures is to assert that *some* of its great myths can throw light on our path; and, in addition, form a common language that transcends *some* of the divisions that cause us to break into factions. The challenge of reflection and judgement can never be set aside.

Living in a Global Society

At the beginning of the twentieth century a group of English-speaking churches came together for a great missionary conference to set out how, in the new century, Christianity would finally become the world's religion and all the other religions on the fringes of 'the civilised world' be made to disappear. Looking back, it seems as naïve as an ambition as the dream – also found then – of building an 'unsinkable ship'. One product of the conference was a magnificent atlas showing where Christianity was established, where it was spreading, and details of the various missionary outposts in 'the Far East', in recently explored Africa, and in other out-of-the-way places.[4] Just as 'civilisation' was spreading outwards along new railways lines to colony after colony, so too was faith. Faith was following the flag – and very often supporting it. Looking back, one is struck by the hubris, the horrors of colonialism, and the blindness of those involved that they did not see that missionaries – whatever their individual intentions – were part of a much larger and darker process. While missionaries sent home stories of the 'black babies saved' and statistics of 'missions established, churches built, and people baptised', they paid little attention to the cultures destroyed, the languages they obliterated, and social survival networks undermined. The missionaries saw themselves as 'simply fulfilling' the so-called 'Great Commission' (Matt 28:19–20). They saw themselves as bringing light into 'darkest Africa' without ever asking what made them link darkness with Africa in the first place. Likewise, they saw themselves as following in the

---

4. H.P. Beach and C.H. Fahs, *World Missionary Atlas* (New York, 1925).

footsteps of Paul and the first 'missionaries' in Acts – a process they saw in the maps in the back of their Bibles which were very similar to the maps they made of their own travels – and that was that! It never dawned on them that Paul came as an equal in culture to the synagogues in which he preached, and that as Christianity spread within the Roman Empire it was often being transmitted by the cultural inferiors of the dominant society and often among the marginalised. The missionary in the modern period arrived as a part of a dominating society where the gospel was the new, improved religion along with railways, firearms, western education, and the colonial District Officer. As recently as the 1980s I asked an Irish missionary who worked in Kenya if he had made a study of the local rituals and beliefs as a basis for a new theological language. What he told me has seared me: 'When I arrive in a compound [note the connotations of the word], the first thing I ask as I get out of the Land Rover [as good a symbol of western technological power as one could get] is whether anyone has been playing with juju [note the cultural insensitivity in the term]. If they have, I tell them to bring it out here, then I sprinkle it with petrol and set it alight.' This may be an isolated incident, but I fear it is symptomatic of what mission has meant to Christians in recent centuries, and still means to many of them.

What is the role of mission in a global society where we need to treasure every human culture and respect each culture as part of our respect for one another and for life? We must adopt an attitude of respectful service: we aim to serve humanity, not to sell our religious ideas. There is no shortage of peddlers of religion, nor any shortage of those who would convert people to any number of philosophies or quick fixes. Peddlers of deceit always have the best, the only way, the truth in a neat box, but disciples are trying to make the lives of all just that bit better, just that bit easier, and just that bit more reflective. We are here as servants of the needy, not as God's sales force. If we are successful as disciples, others may join us and seek out our way – but they will come to us and ask us to help them in their discipleship.

Facing 'X'

There are as many challenges to discipleship today as there are crises we face as human beings. One has only to think of climate change to know that humanity – as a whole – faces problems in nature and extent unlike any we have ever known: and this is a call on Christians, Jews, and Muslims in a special way because we believe that the universe is a creation. We could keep the list going: the communications revolution that has occurred since the arrival of the internet poses questions about how we as human communicate that is transforming what is means to be a disciple. Could we list all these challenges? The simple answer is 'no'. The creation is not a closed system, the future is not determined, we are always going to be surprised. There is always going to be a new situation, let's call it 'X', which will call forth new demands while making older demands redundant. Discipleship is open-ended.

This is a frightening prospect for many people and – given that religion tends to be a conservative force within human societies – it would appear that it is better to imagine 'faith' in conflict with 'modernity'. This notion that the new may be coming, but Christianity is about 'holding-on tight' to the past as 'an anchor' is widely found among those who claim to be 'religious'. This often takes the form that those who are most anxious to be described as Christians are also anxious that there should be 'no change' in 'their' religion, and are often the supporters of reactionary movements in politics. Part of the western dream about religion is that it is 'an unchanging force in a changing world' and so it will find itself in a building with Gothic arches, antique jargon, and filled with grumpy old people who know that the modern world is 'going to hell in a handcart'. Such fearful people may reply, what about the centuries of Christian tradition? I will answer with Picasso's saying: 'tradition is having a baby, not wearing your grandfather's hat!'

Christian faith is that God is with the world now, loves each of us, and in every situation can offer us the light we need for our path. This confidence in the moment is not some simple optimism but is founded upon the living source of all discipleship: it is the Holy Spirit who dwells within us that lights our path forward.

Bibliography

Avis, P., 'The Paschal Mystery and the Church', *Ecclesiology*, 17 (2021), pp. 3–6

Bauer, W., *Orthodoxy and Heresy in Earliest Christianity* (Philadelphia, PA, 1971; original: *Rechtgläubigkeit und Ketzerei im ältesten Christentum*, Tübingen, 1934)

Bauman-Martin, B.J. 'Women on the Edge: New Perspectives on Women in the Petrine *Haustafel*', *Journal of Biblical Literature*, 123 (2004), pp. 253–79

Beach, H.P. and C.H. Fahs, *World Missionary Atlas* (New York, 1925)

Bonhoeffer, D., *The Cost of Discipleship* (London, 1955; original: *Nachfolge*, Munich, 1937)

Boulton, M.M., 'Supersession or Subsession? Exodus Typology, the Christian Eucharist and the Jewish Passover Meal', *Scottish Journal of Theology*, 66 (2013), pp. 18–29

Bradshaw, P.F., *The Search for the Origins of Christian Worship: Sources and Methods for the Study of the Early Liturgy* (London, 2002)

Charlesworth, J.H., *The Old Testament Pseudepigrapha* (2 vols, London, 1983–85)

Chilton, B., *A Feast of Meanings: Eucharistic Theologies from Jesus through Johannine Circles* (Leiden, 1994)

Clark, D., *The Lord's Prayer: Origins and Early Interpretation* (Turnhout, 2016)

De Bruyne, D., *Summaries, Divisions and Rubrics of the Latin Bible* (Turnhout, 2014; 1st edn Namur, 1914)

de Tocqueville, A., *Democracy in America* (New York, 1945)

Ehrman, B.D. (ed.), *The Apostolic Fathers* (2 vols, Cambridge, MA, 2003)

Ely, J.W. and D.P. Jordan, 'Harpers Ferry Revisited: Father Costelloe's "Short Sketch" of Brown's Raid', *Records of the American Catholic Historical Society*, 85 (1974), pp. 59–67

Freedman, D.N. (ed.), *The Anchor Bible Dictionary* (6 vols, New York, 1992)

Furnish, V.P., 'Colossians, Epistle to the', in D.N. Freedman (ed.), *The Anchor Bible Dictionary* (New York, 1992), vol. 1, pp. 1090–96

Furnish, V.P., 'Ephesians, Epistle to the', in D.N. Freedman (ed.), *The Anchor Bible Dictionary* (New York, 1992), vol. 2, pp. 535–42

Glancy, J.A., *Slavery as Moral Problem: In the Early Church and Today* (Minneapolis, MN, 2011)

Kenrick, F.P., *Theologia Moralis* (Mechelen, 1860; earlier edn Philadelphia, PA, 1841)

Kobel, E., *Dining with John: Communal Meals and Identity Formation in the Fourth Gospel and its Historical and Cultural Context* (Leiden, 2011)

Holmes, M.W. (ed.), *The Apostolic Fathers: Greek Texts and English Translations* (Grand Rapids, MI, 1992)

Jones, M., *Feast: Why Humans Share Food* (Oxford, 2007)

Kuhn, T.S., *The Structure of Scientific Revolutions* (3rd edn, Chicago, IL, 1996; first published in 1962)

Laeuchli, S., *Power and Sexuality: The Emergence of Canon at the Synod of Elvira* (Philadelphia, 1972)

Loudovikos, N., *Analogical Identities: The Creation of the Christian Self – Beyond Spirituality and Mysticism in the Patristic Era* (Turnhout, 2019)

Loughlin, G. (ed.), *Queer Theology: Rethinking the Western Body* (London, 2007)

Lowenthal, D., *The Past is a Foreign Country* (Cambridge, 1985)

McGrath-Merkle, C., *Bérulle's Spiritual Theology of Priesthood: A Study in Speculative Mysticism and Applied Metaphysics* (Münster, 2018)

Machielsen, J., *Clavis Patristica Pseudepigraphorum Medii Aevi* (5 vols, Turnhout, 1990–2004)

Martínez, F.G., *The Dead Sea Scrolls Translated: The Qumran Texts in English* (Leiden, 1994)

Marx, K. and F. Engels, *On Religion* (Moscow, 1957)

Metz, J.B., *Faith in History and Society: Toward a Practical Fundamental Theology*, ed. and tr. J.M. Ashely (New York, 2007)

Meyer, M., *The Mithras Liturgy* (Princeton, NJ, 2006)

Meyers, E.M., 'Synagogue', in D.N. Freedman (ed.), *The Anchor Bible Dictionary* (New York, 1992), vol. 6, pp. 251–60

Milavec, A., 'Distinguishing True and False Prophets: The Protective Wisdom of the *Didache*', *Journal of Early Christian Studies*, 2 (1994), 117–36

Murphy-O'Connor, J., *Paul: A Critical Life* (Oxford, 1996)

Niederwimmer, K., *The Didache: A Commentary* (Minneapolis, MN, 1998)

O'Loughlin, T., 'Individual Anonymity and Collective Identity: The Enigma of Early Medieval Latin Theologians', *Recherches de Théologie et Philosophie Médiévale*, 64 (1997), pp. 291–314

O'Loughlin, T., *The Didache: A Window on the Earliest Christians* (London, 2010)

O'Loughlin, T. 'Divisions in Christianity: The Contribution of "Appeals to Antiquity"', in S. Oliver et al. (eds.), *Faithful Reading: New Essays in Theology and Philosophy in Honour of Fergus Kerr OP* (London, 2012), pp. 221–41

O'Loughlin, T., 'From a Damp Floor to a New Vision of Church: Footwashing as a Challenge to Liturgy and Discipleship', *Worship*, 88 (2014), pp. 137–50

O'Loughlin, T., 'Sharing Food and Breaking Boundaries: Reading of Acts 10–11:18 as a Key to Luke's Ecumenical Agenda in Acts', *Transformation*, 32 (2015), pp. 27–37

O'Loughlin, T., *Washing Feet: Imitating the Example of Jesus in the Liturgy Today* (Collegeville, MN, 2015)

O'Loughlin, T., 'The *Protevangelium Jacobi* and the Emergence of the Notion of Consistency as a "Principle" within Christian Theology', in J.N. Bremmer, J. Andrew Doole, Thomas R. Karmann, Tobias Nicklas, and Boris Repschinski (eds.), *The Protevangelium of James* (Leuven, 2020), pp. 206–16

Ortner, S.B., *Sherpas through their Rituals* (Cambridge, 1978)

Otto, R., *The Idea of the Holy* (Oxford, 1923)

Parker, D.C., 'Scripture is Tradition', *Theology*, 94 (1991), pp. 11–17

Parker, D.C., *The Living Text of the Gospels* (Cambridge, 1997)

Raj, A.S., 'Dalits at the Eucharistic Table', *Japan Mission Journal*, 68/1 (2014), pp. 9–14

Reihlen, C., *The Broad and Narrow Way* (London, 1885)

Riesner, R., *Paul's Early Period: Chronology, Mission Strategy, Theology* (Grand Rapids, MI, 1998)

Schiffman, L.H., *The Eschatological Community of the Dead Sea Scrolls: A Study of the Rule of the Congregation* (Atlanta, GA, 1989)

Schwartz, B., 'Memory as a Cultural System: Abraham Lincoln in World War II', *American Sociological Review*, 61 (1996), pp. 908–27

Schwartz, B., 'Christian Origins: Historical Truth and Social Memory', in A. Kirk and T. Thatcher (eds.), *Tradition and Text: Uses of the Past in Early Christianity* (Atlanta, GA, 2005), pp. 43–56

Smith, D.E., *From Symposium to Eucharist: The Banquet in the Early Christian World* (Minneapolis, MN, 2003)

Smith, D.E. and H.E. Taussig, *Many Tables: The Eucharist in the New Testament and Liturgy Today* (London, 1990)

Standhartinger, A., 'The Origin and Intention of the Household Code in the Letter to the Colossians', *Journal for the Study of the New Testament*, 79 (2000), 117–30

Stanton, G.N., *Jesus and Gospel* (Cambridge, 2004)

Troche, F.D., 'Ancient Fishing Methods and Fishing Grounds in the Sea of Galilee', *Palestine Exploration Quarterly* 148 (2016), pp. 281–93

Visser, M., *The Rituals of Dinner: The Origins, Evolution, Eccentricities, and Meaning of Table Manners* (London, 1993)

Weber, T.P., *Living in the Shadow of the Second Coming: American Premillennialism, 1875–1982* (Chicago, 1987)

Wheeler Robinson, H., *The Christian Doctrine of Man* (Edinburgh, 1911; and many later editions)

Wheeler Robinson, H., 'The Hebrew Conception of Corporate Personality',
    Beihefte zur Zeitschrift für alttestamentliche Wissenschaft, 66 (1936),
    pp. 49–62
Yarbro Collins, A., 'Apocalypses and Apocalypticism: Early Christian', in
    D.N. Freedman (ed.), *The Anchor Bible Dictionary* (New York, 1992), vol. 1,
    pp. 288–92

Scriptural Index

Extracanonical Documents

General Index

You may also be interested in:

Worshipping a Crucified Man:

Christians, Graeco-Romans and Scripture in the Second Century

by Jeremy Hudson

By the mid-second century Christian writers were engaging in debates with educated audiences from non-Jewish Graeco-Roman cultural backgrounds. A remarkable feature of some of the texts from this period is how extensively they refer to the Jewish scriptures, even though those scriptures were unfamiliar to non-Jewish Graeco-Romans. In *Worshipping a Crucified Man*, Jeremy Hudson explores for the first time why this should have been so by examining three works by Christian converts originally educated in Graeco-Roman traditions: Justin Martyr's *First Apology*, Tatian's *Oratio* and Theophilus of Antioch's *Ad Autolycum*. Hudson considers their literary strategies, their use of quotations and allusions and how they present the Jewish scriptures; all against the background of the Graeco-Roman literary culture familiar to both authors and audiences. The scriptures are presented as a critically defining feature of Christianity, instrumental in shaping the way the new religion presented itself, as it strove to engage with, and challenge, the cultural traditions of the Graeco-Roman world.

'Jeremy Hudson ... offers important new insights into a significant moment in the development of early Christian thought and of the uses of Scripture – essential reading for all students of early Christianity.'
Judith M. Lieu, Lady Margaret's Professor Emerita, University of Cambridge

Dr Jeremy Hudson studied History at Christ's College, Cambridge. After working for some years in personnel and finance he took an MA (with Distinction) in Biblical Studies at King's College, London and then a PhD at Wolfson College, Cambridge.

First published by The Lutterworth Press, 26 August 2021

Hardback ISBN: 978 0 227 17734 1
Paperback ISBN: 978 0 227 17735 8
PDF ISBN: 978 0 227 90734 4
ePub ISBN: 978 0 227 90735 1

You may also be interested in:

Life in the Spirit:

A Post-Constantinian and Trinitarian Account of the Christian Life

by Andréa D. Snavely

Christians are united in saying that the Christian life is a life in the Spirit. But the unity breaks down when explaining how the Christian life is a life in the Spirit. *Life in the Spirit* is the first book to engage the post-Constantinian critique of the church with the field of Spirit Christology. Building upon the work of post-Constantinians John Howard Yoder and Stanley Hauerwas and upon the Trinitarian Spirit-Christology of Leopoldo Sánchez, this account provides a framework for seeing one's Christian life as one transformed by the Spirit. Snavely rejects the characterisation of life in the Spirit as bringing sinners to faith, and instead proposes that as Jesus lived as the Son of the Father in the Spirit, the Spirit also makes other sons of the father in the image of Jesus. This Trinitarian interpretation shows the Christian life as being one of total trust in God with one's own life, and after death living in Jesus' resurrected life in the Spirit. Snavely's account calls for a reimagining of the church and the Christian life in terms of ecclesial structure, Christian discipleship and the Christian view of marriage. *Life in the Spirit* will not only help Christians to have a better understanding of the place of vocation in the world as witnesses to the lordship of Jesus Christ, but it will also promote unity in the body of Christ based on the actual unity that all his adopted sons and daughters already have by belonging to Jesus Christ's life in the Spirit.

'*Snavely's reimagining of the Church and the Christian life in terms of living in union with the Spirit is to be highly praised.*'
Bradford McCall, in Theological Book Review

Andréa D. Snavely (PhD, Concordia Seminary) is Professor of Bible and Theology at Global University of the Assemblies of God, Springfield, Missouri. He and his wife, Darla, are blessed with a son, Titus, and a daughter, Tessa.

First published by The Lutterworth Press, 29 October 2015

Paperback ISBN: 978 0 227 17552 1
PDF ISBN: 978 0 227 90521 0